Count up

An account of a Bradford childhood in the twenties

by Marjorie Jones

Cover: Dick and Margie aged 3

ISBN 0907734 13 8

First published 1987 by Bradford Libraries and Information Service.

Contents

Chapter One

Security

It was the spring of 1918.

Cocooned in the big, shabby pram, staring at the changing sky through a tear in the hood, Margie thought the world a snug, safe place.

Once she could toddle, that sense of security was shattered, not by the war, of which she remembered nothing, but by frequent abrasive encounters with the uneven flagged steps outside the front door. The pudgy dumpling fell down them at the start of every outing and limped through the next few years with knees swathed in bandages.

Margie's house stood in a long terrace cut out of the hillside. Leamington Street was far enough from the mill and near enough to the park to be respectable. A stunted laburnum fought for existence in the dusty square of grass they called the front garden.

Listers' mill chimney on the hilltop, though a local landmark, couldn't be seen from the house. It was supposed to be the biggest chimney in the world. Georgie said its reinforced top was so big that a horse and cart could stand there. Margie wondered how he knew.

Horse-drawn carts abounded: coalcarts, greengrocers' vans, dustcarts and milk floats. Going home from school, you had to squeeze past them in the narrow, cobbled back street. Margie would sigh with relief on finding it deserted. She would do anything rather than venture within range of a horse's tossing mane. The creatures had a terrifying habit of stamping their hooves or snorting into their nosebags just as you were creeping by.

Her stratagem was either to loiter behind a cart till it had passed her back gate ... a tedious, protracted business ... or to make a dash for it the long way round (that is, by way of the front street and the other end of the back street) in the hope of reaching her gate before the horse did.

It was a big wooden gate with an iron sneck and opened on to a back yard enclosed by high walls. There was no dustbin. Rubbish was put in the ashpit or midden through a trap-door in the yard and raked out once a week into the dust-cart through a similar opening on the street side.

Margie's chubby knees often made painful contact with the patchy concrete of the yard. Two adjoining shabby dark green doors opened off it, one to the house, the other to "the back" or w.c.

"I'm just going' to t' back," one of the grown ups would remark and the intention was understood. The back, also known as the "double-you", was in almost total blackness: you had to grope in gloom for the neat squares of newspaper strung on a nail.

The rented house, strongly built of local sandstone blackened by years of industrial grime, had four storeys or rather three and a half, because of the hill. There was a living kitchen on ground floor level at the back; in front there was only a cellar with a large stone table fixed to the concrete floor and a grating instead of a window. In the frightening "dark hole" under the stairs, which smelt of firelighters, Georgie kept the blawjohn for drawing the kitchen fire.

Except for the one day in the year when the sweep came, a good coal fire burned, winter and summer, in the kitchen grate. The range with its steel fender and polished fire-irons was screened by a tall mesh fireguard with a gleaming brass edge. To the left of the fireplace was the built-in set-pot and under the lace-curtained window the slopstone where you washed up. A large iron mangle with wood rollers occupied one corner. A multi-coloured tab rug, made by Grannie, was spread in front of the hearth.

Besides the large deal table and upright wooden chairs, to which home-made cretonne cushions were fastened with tapes, there were two rocking chairs set one on either side of the hearth. The square one with wooden arms was Grandad's and the low, curved one heaped with cushions, shawls and antimacassars belonged to Grannie. Margie, a compulsive rocker, had bowled them right over on to the concrete floor more than once.

No servants came to answer the row of clapper bells which hung from curved metal springs near the ceiling. Mother and Grannie ran the house between them. In spite of their scrupulous cleanliness there were blackclocks in the kitchen. Keating's powder, the advertised remedy, was ineffective as in a terrace vermin could easily move from one house to another.

Margie never forgot the winter morning when, groping by gaslight for her hairslide which had fallen in the shadow of Grandad's armchair, she picked up instead a shiny black shell with waving spidery legs. It was years before she could recall the incident without a shudder.

2

A flight of uncarpeted wooden stairs led to the first floor. A gate at the bottom prevented Judy, the cat (kept as a mouser, not a pet), from ascending to forbidden regions. It also saved Margie from a damaging encounter with the concrete floor when, true to form, she rolled down the flight from top to bottom.

At the top of these stairs a narrow hallway led to the seldom-used front door. Two doors on the left gave on to what were called, with striking originality, the front room and the back room.

The front room, cluttered with Victorian bric-à-brac, was Grannie's sitting room where she never sat unless there was "company". It was in the back room, their parents' sitting room, that the children played with their toys.

Above these rooms, reached by a more palatial flight of carpeted stairs, were two bedrooms. The front one belonged to Grannie and Grandad. As a small child Margie slept between Mother and Dad in the double feather bed in the back one, with her brother, Dick, three years her senior, in a cot at the side.

This floor also boasted a bathroom with washbasin and bath but no w.c.. As "the back" was two flights away, chamber pots, known as Jerries or Jemimas, were essential items of bedroom furniture.

Another flight of bare wooden stairs gave access to the two attics. Georgie, the children's bachelor uncle, slept in one of them. Apart from his iron bedstead the room contained nothing but a workbench under the skylight where he tinkered at his hobby of watch repairing. Mother's unmarried sisters, Auntie Annie and Auntie Em, slept in the other attic.

With nine occupants the house was overcrowded. For years Dad and Mother had had their names down for a Corporation house. They eventually moved to one in 1926, fourteen years, almost to the day, after their marriage.

Margie was oblivious of the inconvenience and tensions and lack of privacy in the shared household. Alternatively cosseted and reprimanded, scolded and spoiled by so many solid, omniscient adults, she experienced only a comfortable feeling of warmth and security.

Chapter Two

Roots

Grannie had been brought up in a closely-knit rural community. Her father was wheelwright and carpenter in the village of Sherburn-in-Elmet, twelve miles east of Leeds. The region of Elmet dates from Celtic times.

Like many of his family before him, her father was clerk of the village church. Over a period of 24 years he fathered eight children, three sons and five daughters. Grannie, his sixth child, christened Mary but always known as Polly, was born in July, 1846.

Apart from her younger sister, Catherine (Great-aunt Kate whose petit point wool pictures hung on either side of the piano in the front room in Leamington Street), the only other member of the family the children ever heard mentioned was the eldest brother, Great-uncle Henry, a lay preacher. He was pithily summed up as "a Sunday god and a Monday devil".

To hear Grannie talk, everything in Sherburn was wonderful. But when Dick and Margie went there for a day they were disappointed. The Norman church, surrounded by a brood of sombre gravestones, clung to the top of a draughty slope. Across the dusty street lay a small cobbled fold where the relatives lived. It was set about with poky whitewashed cottages which had tiny windows cut into their thick walls. Two things stood out afterwards in the children's minds: the faces of a bewildering crowd of relations and the smell of the primitive earth closet, compared with which the dark double-you at home was the height of luxury.

Grannie must have had an education for she could read the evening paper and did so regularly. She and Great-aunt Kate had been sent to a finishing school where two elderly spinsters taught her English embroidery and her sister petit point tapestry work.

Domestic service was the only career open to them. In the 1860s Grannie left Sherburn for a post in Bradford with a well-to-do family of German origin connected with the wool trade. She was to spend the rest of her life among the mill chimneys of the Industrial Revolution.

Grandad was born on January 21st, 1846, at New Dam in Bowling. His parents had married in 1838 so presumably he was not their first child. His father was a labourer; his mother, who registered the birth, must have been illiterate for she signed the certificate with her mark.

Margie considered the story of the loss of the family fortune highly romantic. She enjoyed recounting a garbled version at school and gloried in the role of erstwhile heiress.

It seemed that Grandad's Great-uncle Purchase (pronounced Percus) Lumley had died intestate with no direct heir to the fortune he had amassed distilling rum, probably with slave labour, at his Dene Valley Dryworks in Jamaica. The estate was put into chancery. The relatives sent out two lawyers to make enquiries and investigations on their behalf but they vanished in suspicious circumstances and were never heard of again. Nor was the Lumley fortune.

Grandad, a distinguished-looking man, had become a woolsorter by the time he met Grannie. Described as the aristocrats of the industry, they were comparatively well paid, though wages in general were abysmally low. In April, 1870, when he was 24 and she 23, they were married in the parish church, later to become Bradford Cathedral.

The marriage produced ten children over a period of 22 years. Only one of them, Victor, died in infancy. The other six sons and three daughters Grannie reared successfully on her husband's modest income, knitting all their socks and stockings herself and making the boys' shirts and the girls' dresses and pinafores as well.

There was little time or money to spare for amusements but every Monday night, after a hard day at the washtub, she would go to the theatre with a women friend, leaving her husband to mind the children. The Prince's Theatre had opened in 1896 with a performance by the Carl Rosa Opera Company. Mrs. Patrick Campbell subsequently played there, while other notable performers like Henry Irving and his leading lady, Ellen Terry, made periodic appearances at the Theatre Royal.

Grannie paid a penny a week for the education of each child. Her eldest son, Harry, was so intelligent that the teacher would beg her to keep him at home for a day or two to let the rest of the class catch up. He suffered from migraine and was grey-haired at seventeen.

Not one of the Lumley children was sent to work in the mill: each was apprenticed to a trade. Arthur and George served their time as cabinet makers and could turn out anything from a violin to a suite of furniture. Walter was apprenticed to a brassfounder, Billy and

Joe trained as French polishers; Annie became a dressmaker and Emily a bookbinder.

The only exceptions were Harry and Nellie. As he was the eldest, Harry had to start earning as soon as he left school. He became a clerk and later an inspector on the tramways before eventually taking the decision to emigrate. Nellie, the oldest girl, had no choice but to stay at home and help her mother run the house.

Apprentices earned no more than pocket money during the seven years of their training and it was for financial reasons that for a time Grandad, assisted by his wife and family, took on a second job, that of curator at the Bradford Library. No doubt also his income had been cut as a result of the bitter nineteen-week strike at the Manningham Mills in 1890.

As a direct result of the strike, the Independent Labour Party was inaugurated in Bradford in January, 1893. Its headquarters came to be known as the Labour Church and there was a Socialist Sunday School in which hymns with new Socialist words were sung to the old Nonconformist tunes. It was thanks to the Socialists who were elected to the City Council that Bradford could boast of the first school clinic, school dentist and school baths in the country.

Harry and his five younger brothers grew to maturity in those idealistic early days of the Labour movement. They attended the Labour Church and became members of the Clarion Cycling Club, named after Robert Blatchford's influential Socialist newspaper.

From a Sunday outing in the Yorkshire Dales they would return home to a generous high tea, bringing with them a troop of friends who well knew that Aunt Polly, as they called Grannie, had a reputation for keeping open house. With one or two of the lads out of their apprenticeship the family was better off now and had moved from Westgate to Spring Gardens, a steeply sloping, tree-lined cobbled street further out from the city centre. No. 27 was a spacious, solid terrace house with a bay window, a front lawn and a large yard at the back. Besides the semi-basement kitchen there were front and back reception rooms on ground level, three bedrooms and a bathroom above, and three attics.

While Nellie tackled the washing up, Emily would entertain at the piano with popular pieces like the Destiny Waltz and "Alice, where art thou?" Arthur could play the fiddle and Harry recited dramatic monologues or humorous sketches from Chambers's Elocution Book. Besides playing on the phonograph cylindrical records of their favourites (Caruso, Melba and Dame Clara Butt), they occasionally attempted to make their own recordings. If a performer finished too soon, someone would rush to the piano, amid screams of laughter, to fill in with a hasty improvisation.

Ballroom dancing and roller skating at the Rink in Manningham Lane were popular Saturday night pastimes. There was no "doing your own thing" about the former. The complicated figures of The Lancers, Cotillion and Quadrille had to be learned pat, and behaviour and dress were strictly formal.

In apprenticing their children to various trades Grannie and Grandad had had in mind the idea of a family factory or co-operative. The Co-operative Wholesale Society was founded not long before their marriage and the movement was gaining momentum. Furniture would be made by Arthur and George and finished by Billy and Joe, the French polishers, and Walter, the brazier. With Annie apprenticed to a dressmaker, Emily trained in leatherwork and bookbinding, and Harry to deal with business and clerical matters, the time for the launching of the family co-operative was fast approaching.

But it was not to be. The fourth son, not yet out of his apprenticeship, told his father somewhat sheepishly that he would have to get married. It is reported that Grandad, astounded and dismayed, summoned all his sons into his presence, arraigned them on the carpet and gave them a good dressing down. That duty done, he ordered them to put their hands in their pockets there and then, and give whatever they could so that the improvident young couple could set up house with at least the bare essentials.

Their child died. The second, Hilda, born in 1900, was taken into their own home and brought up by Grannie and Grandad so that her mother could keep on working at the mill. Her father had been involved in an accident at work in which a fragment of metal lodged in his eye. Hospital treatment proved ineffective and his sight and consequently his craftsmanship were irrevocably impaired. He received not a penny in compensation although for the rest of his life he seemed to be "allus lakin'", as he put it, and in his later years was virtually blind.

Hilda married at twenty and in 1922 set sail with her husband for Australia. She was the third member of the family to emigrate for Harry and Joe, the oldest and youngest of her uncles, had gone before the war. Harry was in his thirties when he went out alone to Western Australia and started sheep farming in a beautiful but isolated spot at Cherry Tree Pool where some of the fields still bear his name. When he was sufficiently established he sent home for his wife, Jinny. His youngest brother, Joe, decided to go out at the same time. A souvenir photograph of the family was taken just before their departure in 1910. Grannie and Grandad never saw Harry or his wife again.

Joe was twenty-one and just out of his apprenticeship when he emigrated. He was a mischievous lad, fo..d of his pint, and regarded as spoilt by older members of the family.

When war was declared he joined up and saw service with the Anzacs in Gallipoli, Egypt and France where he took part in the Battle of the Somme and was lucky to survive. When on leave from the Western Front he always went home to Bradford for a family reunion.

Australian forces were less strictly disciplined than the home-based troops and always ready to take the mickey out of authority. Joe used to spin a yarn about the time he was on leave in the Middle East with a party of Anzacs. They were being shown round a temple where, their native guide informed them with due solemnity, the sacred flame had been burning continuously for hundreds of years.

"Has it now! High time it was out, then!" remarked one irrepressible Aussie and, suiting the action to the word, he extinguished it with a mighty blast. History does not record the sequel.

Early in 1914 what was left of the family in Bradford had quitted the big house in Spring Gardens. By that time both Arthur and Billy had married and set up house. So it was Nellie, the stay-at-home daughter who, with her husband and baby son, moved with Grannie and Grandad and the three unmarried members of the family, George, Annie and Emily, into the house in Leamington Street that was to be their home for the next twelve years.

Chapter Three

Grandad

Both grandparents were getting on for seventy by the time Dick and Margie came on the scene. Their only source of income in retirement was the old age pension of ten shillings a week, together with the money contributed to the budget by the wage-earners of the family.

The children remembered Grandad as a substantial figure with a square grey beard. He wore a cloth cap and steel-rimmed spectacles and usually carried a bundle of books and papers under his arm. He was a great reader and had some interest (not a very profitable one, by all accounts) in a second-hand bookshop. The big mahogany book-case in his bedroom was full of forbidding, musty tomes, most of them antiquated books of travel. He would sometimes take one down and show the children pictures of gorillas and orang-utans, which he called "orange-outangs". In earlier years he had been a collector of guns and still went out occasionally shooting birds or rabbits.

In spite of this surprising trait he was a tender-hearted man and his children, contrary to the prevailing custom, had never been beaten. Mother told a story of how trouble arose among a neighbour's family when she as a child had gone to the house to play. Mrs. Baker had picked up the rolling pin and started chasing her brood round and round the kitchen table. Mother was caught up willy-nilly in this unfamiliar situation. Round and round she ran, terrified. Fortunately, as she approached the back door in yet another breathless circuit of the table, someone coming in opened it and she shot out thankfully to safety.

Grandad had always been particulary solicitous of the welfare of his three daughters. When Mother was in labour with her first child, he could not bear to remain inactive in the house but paced the streets in a state of tension till informed that his daughter was safely delivered of a son, and both mother and child were well.

Aunt Emily, the baby of the family, had a reputation for wildness and had apparently left home on several occasions. Each time Grandad sought her out and brought her back.

Each of the men of the family had a pint pot from which he drank copious quantities of its staple beverage, tea. Printed on Grandad's was the Tyke's Motto, of which he was a living refutation:

"See all, hear all, say nowt;
Eyt all, sup all, pay nowt;
And if ivver tha' does owt fer nowt,
Allus do it fer thysen."

Grandad was a staunch believer in the efficacy of herbs and would consult the herbalist at his shop nearby rather than the doctor. His maxim was, "Everything that grows is good for you," either as food or as medicine. Consequently he was fond of salad in the days before it became popular and would eat quantities of radishes, watercress, lettuce and spring onions from his allotment, with bread and butter for his tea.

One thing he was obstinate about: he would have no truck with insurance. He began to worry somewhat late in the day ... on his deathbed, in fact ... about the lack of provision for his funeral. He needn't have upset himself: Grannie had had them both insured from the day of their marriage and every one of their children from birth. If by any chance Grandad was about when the insurance man called, she would say the neighbours had gone out and left their weekly contribution with her.

The children remembered very well the first time they went away for a holiday. Dad and Auntie Annie took them to Morecambe. Mother couldn't come as her youngest was not yet two and Grandad was ill and confined to bed. As the holiday party said goodbye, Mother was bathing Baby, as she was still called, in the zinc bath on the concrete floor of the kitchen.

Margie, not quite six, was full of rapturous anticipation. Afterwards she retained only confused memories of a train journey in which delight soon turned to boredom; of the unpleasantness of sand between the toes; of rides along the front in a horse-drawn carriage and on something much more hair-raising called the Figure Eight.

The blow fell on Thursday in the form of a bit of yellow paper called a telegram. Grandad had died. They had to cut short their holiday and go home two whole days early.

The house in Leamington Street had an unaccustomed stillness; the curtains were all drawn even though it was still daylight. Grannie kept putting her apron over her face. Margie, busy with her new holiday doll but missing nothing, overheard Mother telling Auntie how Grandad had become delirious towards the end. She said he

10

kept getting out of bed and shouting, "Fetch a bucket of water and some lemons!" and had to be restrained by Georgie.

It sounded very funny to Margie but, as Mother told the story, Auntie Annie sat crying quietly into her hankie.

Chapter Four

Grannie

If it wasn't bronchitis, then it was the rheumatics. But though in winter she was a martyr to one or the other and often bedridden on that account, Grannie ruled the household to her dying day.

The children remembered her as a small, round woman with deep-set brown eyes and white hair pinned back in a bun. She always wore a high-necked blouse, ankle-length skirt and white apron, adding a crocheted shawl when she ventured into the back street to harangue the coalman or greengrocer or to make sure that, on the sweep's annual visit, his brush really **was** sticking out of the chimney-pot. Apart from these excursions she never left the house.

When she was confined to bed, the doctor called frequently. That was on account of her being a private patient and not "on Lloyd George", Mother would observe tartly. Once when Auntie Annie (also a patient of his but only "on the panel") was laid up with a severe attack of 'flu, Mother was furious because he walked straight past the door of her bedroom to pay a visit to Grannie.

Another reason for the doctor's attentiveness, apart from the obvious financial one, was his private resolve to acquire Grannie's corner cupboard. To the rest of the family it was an ordinary enough piece of furniture with plain wooden doors unrelieved by a single fancy pane of glass. But the doctor evidently thought otherwise. He wheedled and flattered and coaxed but all in vain: in Grannie he had met his match. The cupboard had sentimental value for her and she was determined not to part with it.

Most of Grannie's Victorian furniture was crammed into the front room, her sitting room. Crocheted yellow antimacassars complete with tassels covered every inch of the red velvet upholstery: the short curtains which veiled the lower half of the window from prying eyes were dyed regularly with "dolly cream" to match. The carved over-mantel, reaching almost to the high ceiling, was loaded with glass and china ornaments and knicknacks.

Opposite the fireplace stood Grannie's rosewood piano, complete with bracket candlesticks. Auntie Em was the pianist though she seldom bothered to play. But when she was in the mood she would rattle off scales with tremendous bravura before sliding into the haunting strains of some sentimental ballad like "Little grey home in the west".

Auntie Em had vanished by the time Margie was considered old enough for music lessons so a colleague of Auntie Annie's volunteered to teach her. Margie's initial enthusiasm was soon on the wane, especially as no fire was lit in the front room except on special occasions, and her fingers turned blue with the cold. Mother even resorted to locking her in to make her practice, but in vain. After a few desultory attempts she would idle away the time examining the fascinating distractions with which she was surrounded.

Besides sniffing at the pink-ribboned lavender containers which hung on the walls and the pot-pourri in the willow-patterned jar on the piano, she was never tired of fingering the cut-glass lustres on the mantelpiece to set their rainbow pendants tinkling.

The framed petit point pictures worked by Great-aunt Kate hung one on either side of the piano. Their subjects were, of course, religious. One was dominated by the helmeted, scarlet-robed figure of Jephthat of the terrible vow. He stood symbolically grasping his spear as his ill-fated daughter and her maidens, in muted shades of blue and mauve, advanced to meet him with harps and timbrels.

The other depicted the Holy Family. Mary wearing traditional blue, Joseph in a crimson robe and Jesus in a tunic of startling tangerine were grouped in a stilted pose under a tree with dark leaves and exotic golden fruit. An exquisite border of roses and the title in Gothic lettering completed the picture. The delicate texture of the faces, hands and feet had been achieved by splitting the strands of wool and taking minute stitches. Great-aunt Kate must have been a painstaking worker.

The children were fascinated by Grannie's photograph album which they were occasionally allowed to look through. It was so old that even Grannie didn't know who all the sitters were.

It had an embossed dark leather cover which locked with a heavy metal clasp. The gilt-edged pages had yellowed with age and the photographs faded to an insipid sepia. But some joker of the past, probably one of the uncles when a boy, had gone through the book pencilling comments above the photographs and it was these which the children found irresistible.

"What is it?" was the apt superscription over a blurred object that might or might not have been a baby. An undeniably plain young woman with a severe hairstyle and tightly buttoned dark bodice was suitably identified as "Guy Fawks" *(sic)*. But the photograph which amused the children most showed a stocky young couple standing awkwardly together in their Sunday finery, probably on their wedding day. With a fine economy of words the joker had entitled it, "Shufflers Two".

Grannie spent most of her time in the living-kitchen. She worked in it during the day and sat there of an evening in her rocking chair, knitting the inevitable sock. She had to be assisted upstairs to bed; it was Mother who cleaned the house, changed the beds, emptied the slops, brushed the carpets and polished the brass stair-rods.

But in the kitchen Grannie reigned supreme. Every Monday she superintended the lighting of the fire under the set-pot where the whites were boiled, and the possing of the clothes in the dolly tub before they were squeezed through the heavy wooden rollers of the big iron mangle. On a fine day the back yard would be strung with line upon line of cotton twill sheets, striped union shirts and pillow-slips with trailing tapes. Margie was always getting into trouble for dancing in and out of the lines of washing, "dirtying the clothes", as Grannie called it.

Two flat irons were needed for pressing the garments, one heating on the coal fire while the other was in use. It was difficult to prevent smuts settling on the clothes, even though the soot from the fire was carefully blown off the iron before it was inserted into the thin metal "slipper". Articles requiring a hot iron had to be done quickly as it soon cooled down. Margie was occasionally allowed to iron a few hankies but she always complained of burnt fingers in spite of the thickness of the cloth ironholder. The process was so laborious that big things like sheets were never ironed but folded and put through the mangle instead.

On a Friday, baking day, Mother and Grannie were always "fair threng" in the kitchen. Large quantities of white and brown bread and teacakes were baked every week. Grannie, up to the elbows in flour, would turn the big earthenware crock as she worked, slapping half a stone of dough about with nonchalant expertise.

Everything was baked in the oven attached to the kitchen range and heated by the coal fire. Occasionally Mother would try something delicate like a sponge cake but it was almost impossible to gauge the oven temperature correctly.

Rice pudding, which Margie adored, was a rarity. In fact, a sweet course seldom figured on the menu except at the weekend, when there were apple or rhubarb or bilberry pies in season, much loved by the menfolk. Grannie would make a perfect custard tart and then ruin it, in Margie's opinion, by sprinking nutmeg on the top: she regularly got into trouble for trying to scrape it off with her spoon. She also loathed the deceptively pretty caraway seeds which Grannie **would** put in her cakes, and was often scolded for picking out the nauseating little crescents.

In the autumn Mother and Grannie would make, not just one, but five or six spice cakes of various sizes. They were never iced but eaten, according to custom, with a piece of Wensleydale or white Stilton cheese. In the old days when Grannie's sons were all at home, the half dozen spice cakes had usually disappeared long before Christmas and a second batch had to be baked.

A large quantity of mincemeat was made and kept in a great earthenware stewpot. Besides spice cake and mince pieces, the festive fare included jam and lemon cheese tarts, maids of honour, and little buns covered in icing and then dipped in coconut. Margie, ever a "sweet tooth", liked these best of all. But she hated the job, which often fell to her but never to Dick, of rubbing the dried fruit for the cakes and mince pies in a damp cloth and picking out the stalks.

Rabbits were cheap and plentiful. No butcher's or greengrocer's shop was without its row of furry bodies hanging by the feet from a pole outside the door. For Sunday dinner the family usually ate braised rabbit which all the men loved and Margie loathed.

Brisket was more palatable. It was braised very slowly in a big brown stewpot in the oven and eaten cold. There was always Yorkshire pudding to start with, served on its own with gravy.

The family never had a fowl at Christmas. The usual treat was pork, a rarity at other times because of its high price. The main course on this occasion was preceded, not by Yorkshire pudding, but by Grannie's savoury pudding made of breadcrumbs soaked in milk, with the addition of suet, chopped onion, herbs and beaten egg, the whole cooked in a huge greased tin in a moderately hot oven and served with gravy. The idea was to take the edge off the family's appetite before the meat course was reached.

There wasn't much love lost between Grannie and the children. No doubt she was fond of them in her own way but she was an undemonstrative woman and showed them no sign of affection. She never kissed them or put her arms round them; Margie in particular she considered spoilt and faddy. In fact, though they always called her "Grannie", "Grandmother" would have been a more accurate pointer to their relationship, for they were in considerable awe of her sharp tongue and perpetual grumbling.

Surprisingly she was at times susceptible to flattery. The coalman was very obsequious with Grannie so she wouldn't hear a word against him though Mother was convinced that he sold her second grade coal every week at the top price of one and fourpence a hundredweight.

She was a generous woman with everything but praise, and "couldn't abide" housewives who were too stingy to "thoil" good ingredients, or who "stood at t'top o' t' stairs and threw t' currants into t' teacakes," as the saying goes. Nothing but the best, and plenty of it, went into anything she was making.

She would often be heard singing as she went about her work, either well-known hymns like "From Greenland's icy mountains" and "When mothers of Salem", or old folk songs.

She sang "While shepherds watched" to a rollicking hymn tune called Cranbrook which is only associated nowadays with the Yorkshire "anthem", "On Ilkla' Moor baht 'at". It is rumoured that, on a Halifax church choir's annual outing to Ilkley in 1886, two of its members, Mary Jane and her young man, were missing when the rest of the party assembled for the return journey. By the time the courting couple reappeared, rather sheepish and red in the face, the waiting choir had composed and was singing the immortal lines which begin:

> "Whe'er 'as ta bin since Ah saw thee
> On Ilkla' Moor baht 'at?"

As they were supposed to sing only hymns, they kept the letter of the law by singing the parody to Cranbrook.

The children loved the tune with its exhilarating repetition at the end of the verse:

> "And glory shone around,
> And glory shone around,
> AND GLORY SHONE AROUND,"

and never became reconciled to the insipid alternative, Winchester Old, which was currently sung in Sunday School.

Above all else, Grannie was superstitious. You had to knock on wood to ward off ill fortune and must never walk under a ladder. The breaking of a mirror would assuredly bring seven years' bad luck. The dire consequences of spilling salt could be averted only by throwing some of it immediately with the right hand over the left shoulder.

Nothing must be done out of its appointed time. Woe betide the offender who dare sing a note of a Christmas carol outside the Christmas season! This was not, as one might expect, from the first Sunday in Advent to Twelfth Night, but from six weeks before Christmas to New Year's Day.

Grannie's superstitions had their roots in her village upbringing. She was convinced that, if you had the courage to sit alone in All Saints' Church in Sherburn-in-Elmet on All Souls' Eve, you would see pass down the aisle the ghosts of all the villagers who were to die during the next twelve months. It was said that one man who tried it lost his reason.

The finishing school which Grannie and Great-aunt Kate had attended was reputed to be haunted. It was a large house where two elderly spinsters lived alone. Every night after they had gone to bed the row of bells hanging in the kitchen would start a furious clashing and jangling.

Poltergeists, perhaps? Grannie had never heard of such things. But she knew that one night one of the sisters had knelt by her bed and prayed to see the spirit which was causing the disturbance. Then, too frightened to face the ghoulish presence she had conjured up, she leapt into bed and buried her head in the pillow.

Grannie, a practical woman if ever there was one, hadn't much opinion of Margie. She was not a handy child and Grannie considered her totally lacking in common sense. If she were sent to look for anything, she could never find it, though it were staring her in the face.

"Looking with your elbows again!" Grannie would exclaim. "I declare the child is no more use than a book half shut."

She had a fund of similar pithy sayings such as "Wilful waste brings woeful want," and "Two hee-ads are better than one, if they're nobbut sheep hee-ads."

An expert at removing diaphanous strips of peel from apples or potatoes, Grannie tried without success to teach Margie to use a potato peeler. But the child could safely be entrusted to stir a stone jamjar full of lemon cheese in a pan of hot water over the open kitchen fire!

Grannie thought Mother soft because she didn't insist on Margie helping with the housework.

"Once she starts, she'll have a lifetime of it," Mother would reply, thinking bitterly, no doubt, of her own years as unpaid drudge to the household of twelve in Spring Gardens while her younger sisters were out earning money.

Margie came into her own, however, when Grannie's sight began to fail and she could not longer read the dialect stories and jokes (the latter called **Tops and Noils,** a term taken from the wool trade) which the local paper featured on Saturday evenings.

Margie enjoyed the stories and was fascinated by such dialect expressions as "I'm fair capped!" and "Sithee, our Willyum 'Enery! Wheer the hengment hez ta bin?" The tales concerned either T' Owd Maids' Club and its three members, Nancy Knawall, Lizzie Leetfooit and Annie Mation, or the Higginbottam *(sic)* and Nimbletongue families. Mrs. Higginbottam and Mrs. Nimbletongue spent much of their time gossiping over the garden wall about the peculiar behaviour of their respective husbands, Obadiah and Rasmus; the ailments of the twins, Joaseph and Joasephine; and the latest new-fangled notions of their older children, particularly the newly-wed James Walter and his wife, Vi'let.

At school Margie was considered a good reader. As she could get through the stories to her own satisfaction, she offered to read them aloud to Grannie. At first very sceptical of her grand-daughter's prowess, Grannie at last gave a grudging consent and the reading aloud became a regular Saturday night ritual.

Chapter Five

Mother ...

Mother was her parents' sixth child but eldest daughter. On leaving school at fourteen, she was kept at home to help in the considerable task of running the household.

Her two younger sisters went out to work when they were old enough and trained for humble careers. Neither of them ever took over Mother's unenviable job of chief drudge and assistant cook: indeed, Auntie Annie, the lame one, would have been physically incapable of it. But Auntie Em, Grannie's spoilt favourite in Mother's eyes, was never expected to take over the task in her turn.

Mother felt she had never had a chance to develop her talents; the only future open to her was marriage. She had a pleasant voice and had dreamed at one time of going on the stage. But there had been no money to spare for singing lessons so Cinderella was never able to realise her potential. Later on, when most of the family were earning, Grannie managed to afford piano lessons for Auntie Em and this apparent favouritism rankled.

In spite of the drudgery, Mother looked back on the days before her marriage, when her brothers were still at home, as among the happiest of her life.

She was particularly fond of Harry, her eldest brother. He must have been at least ten years her senior, but it was he who ensured that she was included in the energetic social life which he and the second brother, Arthur, enjoyed. With friends of both sexes they went dancing and roller skating, and on Sundays they would set off with the Clarion cycling club for long rides over the county's broad acres.

The correct wear for ladies on these occasions was a costume: that is, a waisted, hip-length jacket and ankle-length skirt in, say, navy serge, worn with a high-necked, long-sleeved white blouse. Boots and a straw boater with a veil completed the ensemble. It must have been very hot in summer.

Women cyclists were, of course, a favourite butt of music-hall comedians and figured in such popular ditties as:

> "There was a young lady of Clewer
> Was riding a bike when it threw 'er.

A butcher came by
Saying, 'Missis, don't cry!'
And he fastened her on with a skewer!''

Bolton Abbey was a favourite rendezvous for the Clarion Club. The Wharfe is shallow and placid enough to be crossed on stepping stones near the ruined abbey itself.

But a mile or two upstream the river has carved its way through the solid rock in a deep, twisted channel where it foams in perpetual tumult. The distance from one bank to the other is only a stride (as its name, The Strid, suggests) and the foolhardy are tempted to try and leap across. The real danger lies, not in the slippery, moss-covered surface of the two obvious footholds, one on either bank; nor in the fact that one of them is higher than the other; but in the treacherous whirlpools which have hollowed out the rock below the surface, and against which even a powerful swimmer is helpless.

Harry and Arthur regularly used to jump, not merely across The Strid but back again as they had, of course, left their bicycles on the other side. Mother would plead with them not to venture but they only laughed, regarding the feat as commonplace, and even tried to coax her into attempting the leap herself. On one occasion Arthur lost his footing on the slimy surface and it was indeed fortunate that strong hands were ready to grab him and haul him to safety.

The young people of the pre-war era were not only cyclists but also, in the words of one of them, J. B. Priestley, "a race of mighty pedestrians". Once Mother and her friend, Emma, wearing their usual cumbersome garments, actually walked in a day from Bradford via Ilkley to Bolton Abbey and back, a distance not much under forty miles.

Few people went away for an annual holiday. The great events of the year were fairs, known locally as tides or feasts. The three biggest in the neighbourhood were Shipley Feast, Manningham Tide and Bowling Tide.

Mother and Emma were experts on that now vanished monster, the steamboat. A large, cabin-type swing covered by a gay awning and powered by a steam engine, it was capable of carrying forty or more on its wooden benches. When fully operational, it would swing on its axis through a semicircle so that, sitting on a bench at one end, you would one moment by lying on your back, and the next hurtling down the length of the, by then, vertical cabin unless you clung for dear life to the mesh of the protective framework.

Mother and Emma would stand in opposite corners at one end of the cabin. Arms firmly hooked in the framework, they would stay on the vertiginous contraption for ride after ride, so absorbed in their conversation that they were unaware when the dizzy rise and fall stopped. Mother had nothing but scorn for folk who went on the steamboat and made a public exhibition of themselves by screaming.

Mother had been an inveterate play-goer before her marriage and the names of the great performers she had seen on tour at the Bradford theatres tripped off her tongue ... Gladys Cooper in "The second Mrs. Tanqueray", Ellaline Terriss, Lily Elsie and, of course, the one and only Henry Irving in "The Bells" and "The Lyons Mail" and in many Shakespearian roles with Ellen Terry as his leading lady. In 1905 Irving collapsed on the stage of the Theatre Royal in Bradford and died later in his dressing room.

Mother also loved musical comedy and knew by heart all the well-loved tunes from shows like "The Quaker Girl", "The Belle of New York" and "The Count of Luxembourg".

At concerts in St. George's Hall she heard the two most famous voices of the day, the crystal soprano of Melba and the dark velvet contralto of Dame Clara Butt.

Mother and her friend, Emma, also patronised variety at the Empire, usually with complimentary tickets issued to Georgie who had a part-time job there as an attendant. Her favourite act was Jack Pleasants, the light comedian whose famous song, "I'm twenty-one today", lived on long after TB had claimed him at an early age. George Formby was also popular though he never attained the fame his son and namesake was to achieve a generation later.

Mother tolerated the broad humour of comedians like George Robey and Dan Leno but expected more modest behaviour of the women. She was critical of Vesta Tilley, the male impersonator; the voluptuous Marie Lloyd and plump Florrie Forde, both of whom she considered cheeky and vulgar; and the skinny Nellie Wallace who invariably came on stage sporting a mangy rat of a fur and simpering, "D'you like my skunk, girls?"

Picture postcards of the beauties of the day were all the rage and Mother had an album full of tinted photographs of Marian Studholme, Gladys Cooper, Vesta Tilley, Lily Langtry and others. They became the pin-ups of soldiers in the First World War.

Mother and Dad met at the Clarion Cycling Club. No doubt Dad was invited home by one of Mother's brothers to sample Grannie's renowned hospitality.

They were a reticent couple, not given to public demonstrations of affection. Years later Margie was to see Dad take Mother's arm when she gave one convulsive sob as they stood together at the grave of their only son who was killed in his twenties in the Second World War. That was the only time she saw them express their feelings in public.

They were married at the Bradford Register Office in October, 1912, at the same time as Uncle Arthur and his bride. After the quiet ceremony they spent a brief honeymoon on the Isle of Man. Dad's family had strong links with the sea and he had once sailed with the crew of a fishing trawler. But Mother was seasick on the crossing and spent most of the honeymoon recuperating.

They came back to live at the house in Spring Gardens with Grannie and Grandad and several unmarried members of the family. They were on holiday in Scarborough with Dick, who was not quite twelve months old, when war was declared on Bank Holiday Monday, 1914.

Besides their son they had three daughters. Margie was born in 1916 and her younger sister in 1920. Their elder sister they never knew: flaxen-haired Mary, pretty as a doll, who was born in February, 1915, and named after Grannie, survived for only eleven months.

Mother was an attractive woman. Small with a rounded figure, good complexion and dark brown eyes, she remained youthful-looking to her death at the age of 77 and her coal-black hair never went completely grey.

All three sisters had long, thick hair which they wore looped elaborately round the head in the fashion of the time. A strange smell of burning filled the back room whenever the visiting (male) hairdresser called to trim and singe it. Came the day when both Mother and Auntie Annie decided to adopt the bobbed style so popular in the twenties and had their hair cut off. There is no record of Grannie's remarks on the triumph of Women's Lib. on this occasion but at the time no-one was left in any doubt of her views.

The children were closer to Mother than to anyone else. There were few demonstrations of affection ... kissing was considered sloppy ... but there was no doubt that Mother loved her children dearly and wanted the best for them. She wished them to have everything she herself had longed for but never obtained, particularly a secondary education.

22

Money was tight: the doctor was called in only on rare occasions ... when the children contracted measles, for example, and when Dick had to have his tonsils and adenoids removed. Even for her confinements, apart from the first one, Mother had managed with the help of an elderly midwife.

Dad and Mother refused to have their children vaccinated against smallpox. Horror stories were circulating about children who after vaccination had developed protuberances like a second pair of ears, gone into convulsions and then died. So they signed the obligatory declaration stating their conscientious objection to vaccination.

Home remedies were the rule: "Kompo for colds" as the adverts declared (and what a nauseating drink it was!); tincture of myrrh rubbed on the gums to relieve toothache, or the external application of the "salt bag" (a cloth bag full of common salt, put in the oven to warm); and Fenning's Fever Cure for just about everything else. The children rather liked "Fennins", a sharp-tasting, colourless liquid that set the teeth pleasantly on edge.

Mother knitted dresses and jumpers for her daughters, and pair after pair of pink or white socks which they wore with black patent leather ankle-strapped shoes. She needed no pattern but, like Grannie, could turn the heel and shape the toe for any size from memory or inspired guesswork.

Occasionally on a Saturday afternoon Mother and Auntie Annie would walk with the children the mile and a half into town to do some shopping. Dad was never able to come on these expeditions as he worked till eight in the evening. At a shop called the Grand Clothing Hall they bought navy reefer coats for winter wear, and blazers and Panama hats for the summer. Mother disliked the pleated gym tunics so many girls wore for school. Her daughters never wore them till they reached the secondary school where they were compulsory uniform.

Except at Christmas, there were seldom sweets or fruit to eat at home. Passing Agars' expensive greengrocer's shop on the way to town, Margie would beg repeatedly but unsuccessfully for some exotic fruit like pineapple. But sometimes on the way home they would stop at a little suburban sweet shop and buy whipped cream walnuts or dairy milk flakes.

Occasionally they went into the market: not the cheap, open-air Flat Iron Market, which Mother scorned to patronise, but one or other of the two permanent markets which, with their high glass roofs, flagged passageways and huge black and gold wrought-iron entrance gates, bore a strong resemblance to railway stations.

In the Rawson Market you could buy meat, fish, cheese, fruit and vegetables. Mother preferred meat from the local butcher but she sometimes bought a rabbit or a piece of Finnan haddock in the market. It was a noisy place where the clatter of boots and shoes on the cobbles and flagstones mingled with the cries of stallholders shouting their wares. The butchers and fishmongers wore navy and white striped aprons and flat straw hats. The fruiterers' assistants, dressed in white overalls, stood beside pyramids of gleaming oranges and red and yellow apples, bawling at the tops of their voices, "Lovely Jonathans! Fresh juicy Jaffas! Come along now! Five for sixpence! Only sixpence for five!"

Nobody shouted in the Kirkgate or Spice Market: a sepulchral calm brooded over most of the stalls. Here you could buy hats and coats, dresses, knitting wools, books and sheet music, flowers and plants. Margie was repelled yet fascinated by the rows of glass cloches covering sprays of artificial white flowers, each one destined for a grave in the cemetery.

At some stalls they sold hot pies and peas. You could go inside and sit on a wooden bench at a scrubbed deal table and drink tea and eat ham sandwiches. The sight of these food counters always made Margie hungry but could never persuade Mother or Auntie to go in. You didn't want folks to see you eating, Mother would say, as though the act were somehow indecent. So a meal in a teashop or restaurant or even a humble market stall was an unknown experience to the children.

Mother and Auntie usually patronised the haberdashery stall which was piled high with handkerchiefs, tablecloths, dusters, paper rolls of bright ribbons, packets of sewing needles and reels of black and white cotton.

The most enthralling aspect of the haberdashery stall was the way the assistants dealt with your money. They popped it, together with the bill, into a little round box which they then screwed into a sort of lid fastened to a wire above their heads. When they pulled a handle the container went spinning away along the wire. It reminded Margie of the Cape to Cairo Railway or the Glen Tramway at Shipley Glen. A few moments later, back came the box in the same strange manner; the assistant would unscrew it, tip out its contents, and hand you your change and the bill just as though the whole magical process were an ordinary everyday occurrence.

Mother and Dad had little free time together as Dad worked such long hours, from eight in the morning till eight at night, including Saturdays, and from noon to two o'clock on Sundays. On a Wednesday, his half-day, he and Mother often went in the evening to the first house at the local cinema. Mother was a devotee of the Pearl White serials in which the heroine, pursued week after week by a fiend called **The Clutching Hand,** was left at the end of each episode in some extreme predicament, either hanging by a frayed rope from the edge of a cliff or tied to the railway line as the oncoming express thundered down the track.

Every Wednesday Margie would beg her parents to take her with them and occasionally her pleas met with success. For her the high spot of the evening was **Felix the Cat** who kept on walking, no matter how hair-raising the adventures he had just survived. He was unable to speak ... the "talkies" hadn't yet arrived ... but every child knew by heart the words and music of his popular song.

> "Felix kept on walking, kept on walking still.
> With his hand behind him you would always find him.
> Blow him up with dynamite but him you couldn't kill!
> Miles up in the air he flew;
> He just shouted, 'Toodle-oo!'
> Landed down in Timbuctoo, and kept on walking still."

Margie loved the occasional brief fashion films. Mauve and green lights played on romantic ladies draped in frilly tea-gowns or gleaming evening dresses. Wearing round their sleek heads that emblem of the twenties, the Suzanne Lenglen bandeau, and waving ostrich feather fans, they slipped gracefully from one languid pose to another.

The feature films were usually melodramatic and often downright terrifying. They were silent, of course, and as the captions were inadequate, it was often difficult to follow the plot. Appropriate music, either soulful (Hearts and Flowers) or dramatic (Overture, Poet and Peasant) was played continuously by the hardworking piano accompanist.

Mother and Auntie took the children to a matinée in town to see the one and only Rudolf Valentino in "The four horsemen of the Apocalypse", a famous film about the war. It was screened no more than five years after the Armistice. Valentino portrayed a wounded soldier with his head heavily bandaged. In one vivid sequence an odious German general, obese, helmeted and covered in foam, was shown sitting at his ablutions in a beautiful gold filigree bath in a captured French chateau. Obviously the producer had no intention of sowing any seeds of reconciliation.

In summer there were occasional Sunday walks to Northcliffe Woods in Shipley where one could scuff along happily, ankle-deep in a carpet of soft pine needles; or out beyond Heaton Woods to a farm made famous by its enigmatic sign, "Six Days Only".

But Manningham park was the favourite spot and the family seldom went further on Saturday afternoons. Dick soon became too high and mighty to be seen in the company of anyone but other boys, so Mother and Auntie Annie, with Baby in the pram and Margie skipping ahead in imminent danger of yet another tumble, would make for their favourite seat along a quiet, tree-lined path.

In the summer a brass band played in the park on Sunday afternoons and evenings. Several large metal collecting boxes mounted on legs were placed at each entrance and manned by attendants selling programmes. Some folk passed by without contributing, whether they planned to go near the bandstand or not. Mother thought this very brazen and always paid for a programme, though she grumbled that the music could scarcely be heard from the secluded corner she and Auntie favoured. Margie loved to put the penny in the box and hear the clatter as it dropped on to the pile of coins.

Occasionally they walked along to the bandstand but never went into the enclosure where seats cost threepence and sixpence. Margie didn't understand the music, stirring and plaintive by turns, but she admired the bandsmen in their smart uniforms. Military bands like those of the Coldstream and Grenadier Guards paid regular visits each season; so did the famous Black Dyke Mills Band from neighbouring Queensbury, winners of many a national competition.

Margie always read through the programme though it was full of long words she didn't understand:

> Overture, Zampa, by Hérold
> Selection, Rigoletto, by Verdi
> Intermezzo, Cavalleria Rusticana, by Mascagni

Mother seemed to know all the tunes and would hum familiar passages under her breath.

The soprano soloist's shrill invitation to the **Chocolate Soldier** was blown away on the wind and could scarcely be heard beyond the enclosure, but one could hardly fail to be aware of the bass-baritone's full-blooded yearning for the **Road to Mandalay.** And towards the

26

close of the evening it was customary for the soloist to lead the audience in the singing of a well-known hymn like "Abide with me" or "The day Thou gavest".

Chapter Six

... and Dad

A tall, spare, clean-shaven man, Dad would have been handsome had his grey eyes been less prominent. The children couldn't believe that his straight dark hair had been red enough in his boyhood to earn him the nickname, Carrots. Though, like the other men of the family, he wore the plebeian cloth cap for work, he looked very smart at the weekend when dressed up and sporting a billycock.

His children were a bit afraid of Dad, possibly because they so seldom saw him. He had set off for work before they came downstairs in a morning and, in their younger days at least, they had gone to bed before he returned at half-past eight.

When he was only eight his father's confectionery business had failed and he had been sent round from door to door selling teacakes. That had marked the end of his regular schooling.

There was little contact with Dad's relatives who lived in Hull and Grimsby. The children were surprised to discover that they had a second grandfather. They met him only once. He was a widower, grey-haired and moustached and wearing the navy and scarlet uniform of the Salvation Army. One of his sons began, but never completed, a course of training for the Congregational ministry.

Besides their church connections, Dad's family had strong links with the sea. Large portraits of two young men in the uniform of the Royal Navy hung on either side of the fireplace in the back room in Leamington Street. They were Dad's cousins who had perished at sea during the war. One of his brothers became skipper of a trawler and was awarded the M.B.E. for minesweeping services with the Merchant Navy during the Second World War.

Dad himself went to sea on a fishing trawler when he was old enough to leave school but one trip was enough for him. His second job, equally short-lived, was in a slaughterhouse where, not surprisingly, he found the work repugnant.

After his trial apprenticeships to the fish and meat trades, Dad settled down as assistant in a grocer's shop in downtown Bradford. Apart from two years on active service in the First World War, he spent the rest of his life there. In spite of his sketchy schooling he wrote

Father *(second left, bottom row)*

a fair hand and his Arithmetic was excellent. After many years of service to the proprietor (service as devoted as if the shop had been his own) he was given the opportunity of buying the goodwill, a chance he richly deserved. The shop was his world, and his delight in owning the small business must have been intensified by boyhood memories of struggle and penury.

A quiet man with no inclination for soldiering, he was conscripted into the army in 1917. A photograph of his platoon showed him sitting erect and smart in his khaki uniform, hat straight on head, arms folded, trousers swathed in ugly puttees from knee to ankle.

On the back of the photograph Dad had pencilled a note to Mother:

"My dear wife,
Just a few lines hoping they will find you all in good health. Well, dearest, I don't think much of the photo. What do you think? I feel really bad today. I have not been out of the hut and some of the chaps have had to go to bed. You see, they gave us a double dose this time. We are supposed to be on 48 hours rest, but if any officer comes in and sees you are not doing anything, they soon find you a job, it doesn't matter how ill you feel. In fact, I can hardly walk about today. With all my love and kisses to yourself and Dicky and Margie, from your loving husband, Harold."

The double dose of injections was followed by embarkation for the Middle East. Dad considered himself fortunate to be sent there rather than to the Western Front. All the same, the war nearly cost him his life.

When Margie was still a baby, a yellow envelope addressed simply to "Mary" (Mother's first name which she never used) was delivered to the terrace house below the mill. On Grandad's insistence Mother opened the telegram to learn that her husband was seriously ill with malaria somewhere in the Middle East. Fortunately he recovered but the severe attack was followed at intervals by others, including a particularly bad one more than ten years later.

There was always a bottle of quinine, the standard remedy for malaria, in the house. As far as Dad was concerned, it was also the sovereign remedy for everything else and, when **he** was around, the children were dosed, not with Fenning's, but with quinine.

Dad was reticent about his wartime experiences in India, Palestine and Mesopotamia. Occasionally the few relics of his travels would be taken out of the drawer where they were stowed away, and shown to the children. Carved in relief on a satin-smooth section of cedar wood was the profile of a sorrowful man with long hair. There were pressed flowers from the Garden of Gethsemane and a rosary of wooden and mother of pearl beads on a chain.

Unlike Uncle Bill, Dad never recounted gloomy tales about the war. But one amusing story the children never tired of hearing was the chestnut about passing communications down the line. The message, "Send reinforcements: we're going to advance" degenerated in course of transmission to "Send three and fourpence: we're going to a dance."

On rare occasions Dad might be heard singing such wartime hits as "Pack up your troubles", "Tipperary" and his favourite, "Goodbye-ee!" The song that intrigued the children most listed the officers and other ranks in order of seniority, but they never found out the nature of the message passed from the colonel to mademoiselle from Armentières.

> "What was the tale the colonel told the adjutant?
> What did the adjutant say to Major Brown?
> What did the major whisper to the captain?
> The captain told the sub. to pass it down!
> What did the quartermaster tell the sergeant?
> The sergeant told the corporal, it appears;
> The corporal told the private and the private told his gal:
> Now she's looking for mademoiselle from Armentières!"

Dad still wore his army belt with the brass letters "M.G.C." for Machine Gun Corps. Other wartime mementoes were the faded photographs, taken in the Middle East, of Dad and the rest of his gunnery crew. The one Margie liked best was a studio portrait of him looking very dashing in khaki shorts with his sun helmet on his knee.

Dad was devoted to his work and couldn't have taken more pride in the grocer's shop, had it belonged to him. He yearned for his own business and was convinced that with a hundred pounds capital to buy the goodwill of some little corner shop, like the one where he worked, he could make his fortune. Alas! a hundred pounds, a small sum by present-day standards, was an unattainable dream to a married man with three children to support on little more than three pounds a week. He was fifty before his opportunity came but he made the most of it and wanted nothing better from life.

Mr. Smith's shop was in a downtown neighbourhood on a corner near Valley Parade football ground where two narrow, cobbled, hilly streets converged. Besides groceries it sold potatoes, bread, sweets and cigarettes, brushes, dusters, overalls and stockings. As the premises were also licensed for the sale of beer, wines and spirits, they were open from 8 a.m. to 10 p.m. every day of the week except Wednesday, which was early closing day, and Sunday. Even on early closing day the shop was open from eight to ten in the evening because of the licence, while business hours on Sundays were from twelve to two, and from eight to ten. Although Dad normally left for home at eight o'clock, he would work till ten if his employer wanted to go out for the evening, and he always turned in on Sundays from twelve till two.

The shop was spotless: every day Dad yellowstoned the worn doorstep. From a wooden trap-door in the causeway outside one of the shop windows, steep stone steps led down to the beer cellar. When the brewer's dray arrived, the trap-door was lifted, a wooden plank was placed across the steps, and the barrels of draught beer were rolled down to Dad waiting in the cellar. Small wonder he was so thin that he looked hollow!

His employer's income was augmented on several occasions due to Dad's initiative. When there was a football match, a long queue would form in Holywell Ash Lane as people moved slowly through the turnstiles into the ground. It was Dad's idea to set up a stall outside the shop, under a large umbrella in Bradford City's claret and amber stripes. In reasonable weather he did a roaring trade in crisps, sweets, soft drinks, chocolates and cigarettes.

As Easter approached, Dad would start taking orders for decorated eggs. He was a dab hand with icing. Using the know-how gleaned from his father's short-lived confectionery business, he embellished the chocolate eggs with pink and white roses, stars, waves, loops and squiggles. The recipient's name was written in icing in a beautiful longhand across the middle of each egg, and flowers, silver balls, chickens and tiny eggs were added. Orders came pouring in and were meticulously recorded so that no two completed eggs looked alike. If Dad were pressed for time he would ride home from work at the weekend on the heavy shop bike with its delivery basket full of cardboard cartons of eggs, and do the decorating in his own time. No doubt Mr. Smith's financial reward from the enterprise was considerably more than Dad's.

Mr. and Mrs. Smith were a stout, genial couple, fond of social occasions. Mr. Smith owned a little Jowett and belonged to a motoring club, for in the early days of the sport it was the fashion to go for a run en masse.

One Sunday the family was informed that Mr. Smith was coming round in the Jowett after dinner to take some of them out for a drive. This was an unheard-of treat for none of them had ever been in a motor-car.

Dad must go, of course, sitting in state in the front seat beside Mr. Smith. The other two places were in the dickey seat, an uncomfortable upright perch with a straight back formed from the open lid of what was nothing more than a boot.

The adults showed their wisdom by allowing Dick and Margie, much to their surprise, the privilege of going for a ride in the dickey seat. Its delights soon palled. It was uncomfortably cramped, even for two children: obviously Mr. and Mrs. Smith never sat there. It was also extremely cold. Dad and his boss were protected from the elements by the flapping canvas roof, behind which the two children sat bolt upright in summer clothes and blazers, without even a rug to protect their bare knees from the wind that whistled round them.

The twenty-mile-or-so journey to Skipton must have taken well over an hour. By the time they got there, Margie's mind was filled with only one thought: that of relieving her uncomfortable condition. But it was difficult for a shy little girl in the company of three males to draw attention to this delicate subject.

As Mr. Smith walked them up and down the deserted market-place, expatiating on how crowded and colourful it was on market days, Margie, looking with her elbows as usual, desperately scanned the horizon for any sign of a public convenience. So the journey home was for her one long cold agony.

Margie's other memory of Mr. Smith was a happier one. He and his bachelor son, an engineer who subsequently patented several inventions, made a doll's house for her sixth birthday.

She was quite overwhelmed on being shown this unexpected present. The large house was double-fronted with a tiny green lawn on either side of the sandpaper path. Clothes pegs, cut short and varnished, made realistic gateposts. The two storeys were not subdivided into rooms so there was plenty of scope for moving the furniture about.

And what furniture! Each large, hand-made wooden piece was decorated with pokerwork. The bed was five or six inches long, big enough to hold a sizeable doll, and there was even a rocking chair, much to Margie's delight. Auntie Annie must have been let into the secret for the pillows and bedspread and the pretty net curtains at the windows had certainly not been made by two men.

Margie's pleasure in the substantial gift was surpassed, if that were possible, by Dad's gratification that his employer and his son should have gone to so much trouble over a present for his little girl. Nobody observed that perhaps Mr. Smith was paying a little of the debt he owed his devoted employee.

The back room was the one the children liked best. They played there when they weren't at school or in the living kitchen. Their toys and dolls, including the doll's house and Dick's rocking horse and toy fort, had a special place. Grannie's famous cupboard occupied one corner, while on either side of the fireplace hung the head-and-shoulders portraits of Dad's sailor cousins who had been drowned in the war. A shabby dark paper patterned with peacocks covered the walls, and the armchairs and sofa were upholstered in embossed green velvet.

On Sunday evenings in winter, when the coal fire had been specially lit, the children and their parents, often joined by Auntie Annie, would gather round the big square table to play simple card games like Snap and Old Maid. The latter was a type of Patience in which one card was hidden under the bobble-fringed chenille cloth and the player left with its counterpart at the end of the game was the Old Maid.

Most popular of all was Housey-housey, described on its box as Lotto, but familiar today under the name, Bingo. Each player was given a card with a selection of numbers on it, from one to ninety. The caller drew numbered counters from a drawstring bag, shouting them out as fast as he could, and the first player to cover up all his numbers was the winner.

Dad, who had seen the game played in the Army, called out so fast that one could easily miss a number. To make it more difficult, he also used soldiers' jargon.

"Kelly's eye," he would rattle off, "medicine and duty, clickety-click, top o' th' house, legs eleven", and so on.

Kelly's eye was number one; clickety-click, sixty-six; and top o' th' house, ninety; but Margie could never remember which number was medicine and duty, and its crude meaning escaped her completely.

Sometimes, as a treat, Dad would put on the gramophone. It wasn't the really old-fashioned kind with a huge horn, like the one old Uncle Arthur still had, but you had to wind it up by hand and change the needle for every record.

The children knew the records by heart; few were suitable for them. It was often difficult to catch the words of the "vocal refrain", as it was described on the label.

The most dramatic record was undoubtedly Balfe's famous setting of Longfellow's poem about a youth who, for some unexplained reason, **would** ascend a dangerous mountain towards nightfall, grasping a banner in his hand to make things even more difficult. It was very affecting, especially at the end when his lifeless but beautiful body had been found by a faithful St. Bernard dog, and a choir of heavenly voices sang a fast and furious "Excelsior!" over and over again.

It was almost impossible to get all the words, and for years Margie was mystified as to why the youth should have been "grasping in his hand **a vice**", presumably like the heavy metal one clamped to the stone table in the cellar. He was, of course, grasping (the banner) in his hand of **ice**!

The family also possessed something called the **wireless**. It was a crystal set. Dad had to tinker about for ages with the **cat's whisker** to get the programme at all, and then everybody had to keep quiet so that those wearing headphones could listen in.

The children didn't like being quiet nor did they enjoy listening in as the headphones were heavy and uncomfortable. But a few years later a marvellous innovation made all the crystal sets obsolete. On the new valve set you could hear the programme without wearing headphones at all.

Occasionally on a Sunday evening Dad would take the children with him to the Congregational chapel down Oak Lane. The vast building had three separate galleries and family always sat on the front row of the one on the right. Fortunately, Dad wasn't against the eating of sweets in chapel, and would put his hands in his pockets and produce a few toffees to help everybody through the sermon. Even so, the final hymn, usually of a lively nature like **Thou whose almighty word** or **Fight the good fight,** came as a welcome relief.

Auntie Annie went occasionally to St. Luke's Anglican church just across Leamington Street. All the children had been christened there although Mother never attended church or chapel, being of the opinion that most of those who did were hypocrites.

Nevertheless the children were sent regularly to the Anglican Sunday School. Dick was disgusted at being taught by a woman. The unfortunate Miss Ayrton, an attractive young lady with long auburn hair fastened in a bun, was known to her class of unruly small boys as Miss Hairpins.

When it was Margie's turn to be initiated, she refused to attend Sunday School at all without the moral support provided by Topsy, a floppy black doll whose smart yellow dress and cap had been knitted by Mother. All went well till one of the boys pulled the jaunty green pompon on Topsy's cap. The insult to Topsy seared Margie's soul; she would not be pacified and the teacher had to escort her home, there and then, in a state of shock. How she was persuaded to attend future sessions history does not record, but attend them she did ... until her obsession with the star card.

This enviable possession belonged to Margie's friend and contemporary, Jack Ambler, who lived across the back street. It was a stiff blue card, folded in two, bearing his name and address; inside there were rows and rows of pretty blue stars. And every time he attended St. John's Wesleyan Sunday School another blue star was stamped in it.

Nothing would now suit Margie but the possession of her own star card. She nattered Mother until eventually she was allowed to forsake the church and go to the Wesleyans with Jack on Sunday afternoons. Perhaps Mother took into account the fact that the Wesleyan chapel, which observed Anglican Morning Prayer, was, as folk said, "church in a morning and chapel at night".

Then Dad put his foot down. He was not usually home on Sunday afternoons as, after his twelve to two stint in the shop, he would go to the Brotherhood meeting at the Salem Congregational Mission near by. So it was some time before he found out that, while two of his children were being brought up as Anglicans, the third had become a Wesleyan Methodist. He decided that all three had better be Congregationalists like himself.

None of the children liked the idea. The Sunday School he wished them to attend was attached, not to the chapel near home where he went on Sunday evenings, but to the distant Salem Mission in Queen's Road where the Brotherhood meetings were held. The fifteen-minute uphill walk home from the new Sunday School was a tiring drag, especially for Baby who was only five at the time.

The Brotherhood meeting, held in a large semi-basement room, began and ended fifteen minutes later than Sunday School. Sometimes the children would decide to wait for Dad; the walk home didn't seem as long and dreary when he was there. They would peer down through the railings, trying to see into the room as the rollicking strains of "Sound the battle cry!" or "When the roll is called up yonder, I'll be there!" burst from several hundred lusty throats.

The meeting concluded with the singing of the special Brotherhood song, set to the tune of "Men of Harlech". It culminated in the rousing chorus:

> "Hail our brotherhood foundation!
> Hail our holy federation,
> League of service and salvation!
> Love to each and all!"

Dad talked a lot about the marvellous Christmas party which was given each year for the children, so it was anticipated eagerly. But though there was a huge, splendidly decorated tree hung with presents, the gifts themselves were paltry.

The Anglican Sunday School treat in the summer had been better value, even though it started unpromisingly with a short service in church. After singing "Onward! Christian soldiers", a suitable prelude to an excursion, the spruced-up children were herded into specially cleaned-up coal carts. Margie thought the line in the hymn, "Like a mighty army moves the Church of God", must refer to coal carts full of children. Huddled close together, they submitted to, rather than enjoyed, the bumpy journey to a distant field where mugs of tea and long buns were distributed.

Dad was an excellent swimmer and played water polo for his club, the Bradford Dolphins. He was also an expert oarsman and in the summer would take the children in a rowing boat on the park lake, feathering the oars so delicately that they barely skimmed the surface of the water.

On Monday evenings in winter Dad and Dick would go to the swimming baths in Drummond Road, returning home about half-past nine. Margie proclaimed Monday as "staying-up night" because Dick was out so late. When ready for bed, she would sit reading quietly in a corner of the living-kitchen, hoping that no-one would notice her. Grannie disapproved of children staying up and was all for packing her off to bed, but Auntie Annie always took her part.

The great attraction on Monday evenings was the newly-arrived comic, **The Rainbow**. Margie devoured the unlikely adventures of Tiger Tim and the other seven Bruin boys, and the even less credible activities of Bonnie Bluebell who possessed a good stock of riddles and a pair of Magic Gloves.

But her favourite character, without any doubt, was Sunshine Susie. It was her appearance, rather than the adventures of her two stupid Pomeranian dogs, that attracted Margie. She was pretty, which Margie was not; she wore her hair in the long ringlets Margie was never allowed to have; and she was so grown-up that she wore court shoes with high heels.

At the age of nine Margie discovered **The Magnet** to which Dick had progressed some time before. She succumbed entirely to the fascination of Greyfriars, its boarding establishment for boys, where the most heinous sins you could commit were smoking behind the quad and having a flutter on the gee-gees. It was all Greek to Margie but she accepted without question the standards of her heroes: Harton Wharton, the juvenile lead, and his chums, the Famous Five of the Remove, whose conversation consisted in the main of exclamations like "Great Scott!", "Cheeky ass!" and "Hello, hello, hello!" She was less interested in the character parts: Vernon-Smith the Bounder; Coker, the silly ass of the Fifth; the American Fisher T. Fish; the somnolent though good-natured Lord Mauleverer; and Billy Bunter in checked trousers and too-tight jacket, stealing other fellows' tuck while awaiting his ever-delayed postal order and, when caught out, indulging in such fearsome expressions as "Yarooh!" and "Leggo, you beasts!"

Mother was just as keen on **The Magnet** as her two elder children; the three were equally unscrupulous in their efforts to bag the popular journal the minute it came through the letter-box.

During vacations the stories moved from the restricted milieu of Greyfriars and the jurisdiction of Dr. Locke, the Head, and Mr. Quelch, the form-master of the Remove. The Famous Five visited India, the homeland of one of their number, Hurree Jamset Ram Singh, the Nabob of Bhanipur, known affectionately to his friends as Inky, and the originator of such phrases as "The delightfulness is terrific" and "The cracked pitcher is the bird in hand that spoils the broth."

They holidayed in Kenya with a faithful guide and mentor, Kikolobo, reminiscent of Bosambo in Edgar Wallace's **Sanders of the River** books. One Christmas they even became involved in a who-dunnit at Wharton Lodge where the baddy was finally revealed as Packington, the too perfect new butler from Australia.

The only character to rival Harry Wharton in Margie's affections was the handsome and virtuous George Wingate. He was regularly ousted from his position as head of the school by Gerald Loder the cad, another member of the mighty Sixth. But virtue always triumphed in the end.

As has been said, Dad and Mother used to go to the cinema on Wednesday evenings. Sometimes Dad would decide to go further afield than the Oak Lane cinema. The Marlborough near the day school, a ten-minute walk away, was superior because it had a circle. Another of its attractions was a stall nearby where a man in a white coat and flat straw hat sold such delicacies as hot pies and peas, polony, black puddings, tripe and udder. Margie had no idea what part of the animal's anatomy the latter was and called it "hudder".

Occasionally Dad was persuaded to buy something from the stall for supper. Margie was bitterly disappointed with her first taste of that much-acclaimed northern delicacy, tripe. In contrast with the slimy dishcloth feel of tripe, the taste and texture of hudder were delightful, provided one didn't dwell too much on its origin.

Fish and chips were a rare treat. Dad sometimes bought them for supper after an evening at the pictures, if he were feeling particularly generous. Mother could never afford them for the whole family as a "fish and a pennorth" (of chips) cost all of fourpence. The first time Margie experienced the delight of a fish and a pennorth for supper, she was instructed to eat plenty of bread and butter with it. Anxious to oblige, and with an eye to similar treats in future, she dutifully ate so much bread and butter that she hadn't room for all the main delicacy.

Chapter Seven

Pig in the middle

"There's a present for you both downstairs," Auntie Annie had said one morning.

That was odd, because it wasn't anyone's birthday. Dick had had his presents a fortnight earlier when he reached seven, and two weeks before that, Margie had celebrated her fourth birthday, though she didn't remember much about it.

It was also odd that **Auntie** should be getting them up. That was something Mother always did. As she helped Margie pull on her socks and button her ankle-straps, Auntie went on talking in an excited sort of way.

"What do you think it is? You can both have a guess."

Dick plumped straight off for a football. Margie could only think of a doll. Her guess was the nearer, but the announcement that they now had a baby sister meant nothing; it was outside the bounds of their experience.

They were struck more by the strangeness of the situation than by anything else. For downstairs in the back room, where normally they played with their toys, a bed had mysteriously appeared. What was more, sitting up in it, wearing a nightie and with her hair hanging round her shoulders, though it was long past her getting-up time, was Mother. In her arms, its face just peeking above the bedclothes, was what looked like the doll of Margie's guess, wearing a frilly cap.

The arrival of Baby was a mixed blessing as far as Margie was concerned. Dick as the eldest still did everything first and got any treats that were going. But now there was another rival who had to be favoured because she was the **youngest.**

"Let Baby have it!" and "Give it to Baby!" were the most objectionable words Margie had ever heard. What was worse, Baby continued to be treated as one long after she was old enough to be called by her baptismal name.

Margie remembered the christening well because she and Baby were baptised at the same time, the ceremony presumably having been omitted four years earlier. It took place one evening in St. Luke's church just across the road, in the presence of several uncles and aunts. Afterwards she sat by the fire in the kitchen trying to rub away the wet mark made on her forehead by the man in the long white dress.

Margie's best doll, so precious that she was rarely played with, was Brenda. Her blue eyes, fringed with real lashes, opened and shut; she had real hair; her arms and legs were jointed so she could sit up; and when you turned her over, she said, "Mamma". Her beautiful clothes, a white lawn petticoat with lace insertion in a Greek key pattern, a white silk dress with tucked bodice and lace trimming, and a hooded cloak of blue velvet lined with white silk. Her home was a large fawn pram, just like a real baby's pram, with padded seats and a waterproof hood and cover.

The day inevitably dawned when Baby, too, wanted to play with Brenda and it had to be made plain to the possessive Margie that, as buying another expensive doll and pram was out of the question, ownership must henceforward be joint. Being "pig in the middle" was a hard life.

When Mother and Auntie decided to have a studio portrait of the children taken, Baby, who was three, took a violent dislike to the idea. All the while they were getting ready and all the way to the studio, she insisted that **she** wasn't going to be in the picture. She was finally pacified by the assurance that she was there merely to keep the other two quiet.

She was placed on a high-backed chair with Dick and Margie standing one on either side. Fidgeting peevishly, she eyed with disapproval the photographer who kept disappearing under a black cloth and telling her to watch for an elusive dicky-bird.

"I'm only here to keep them pyet," she reminded him with severity.

The photograph turned out surprisingly well. Margie was wearing her best dress of brown serge, made by Auntie Annie, with an embroidered linen collar and a skirt consisting of separate panels trimmed with braid. Her short straight har was taken severely back into a huge bow of broad ribbon.

Dick, handsome as ever in jersey and knitted tie, short trousers, knee-length stockings and boots, stole the picture as usual with his engaging crooked smile, so like Mother's.

Between them squirmed the fly in the ointment, the impish figure of Baby with her shock of short fair hair and enquiring expression.

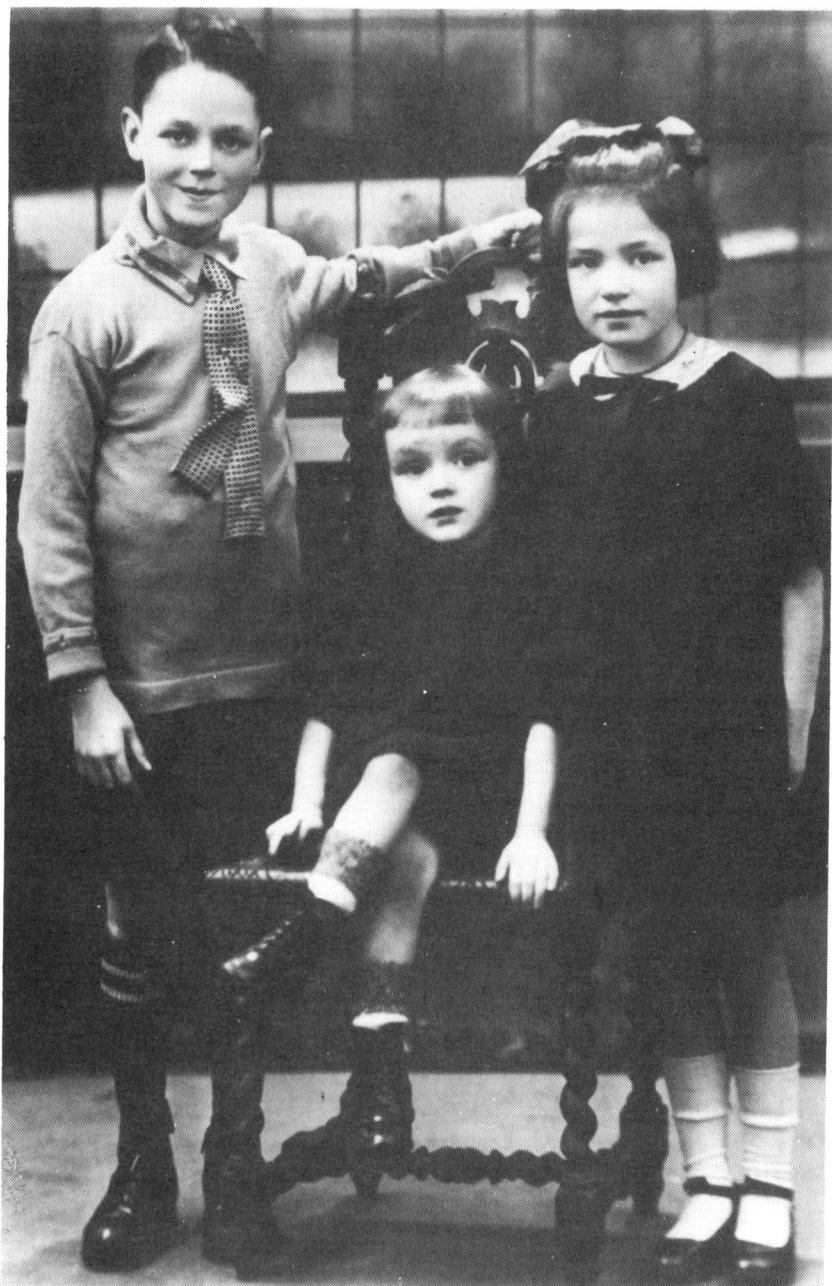

Dick, Baby and Margie

No doubt she was insisting once again to the harassed photographer as the camera clicked: "I'm only here to keep them pyet!"

At Drummond Road Board School Dick was regarded as one of the best pupils. He learned morris dancing, became a class monitor and was a member of a children's choir that sang "God bless the Prince of Wales" when that phenomenally popular young man paid an official visit to Bradford on 20 May, 1923.

> "Better lo'ed ye canna be ...
> Will ye no' come back again?"

they implored as his motorcade vanished from view among the bobbing heads of a vast throng that had gathered in Manningham park in hopes of catching a glimpse of him.

One wet day during the holidays a school friend came to play with Dick. He was a thin, lanky boy with protruding ears and straight fair hair brushed back from a narrow forehead. After they had examined Dick's cigarette cards ... flags of the nations, optical illusions, the world's children and a beautiful pop-up set of birds' eggs ... the two graciously allowed Margie to take part in an improving game called "Who knows?"

Each player in turn took a slip of card at random from a draw-string bag and asked the others the question he found there. The winner was the first one to cover all the blank spaces on his large card with correctly answered slips.

Margie wasn't doing at all well with questions like "What is lapis lazuli?" and "Where is the eastern terminus of the Trans-Siberian Railway?" and, apart from a few spellings, her card remained obstinately blank.

The tables were turned later when, thirst for knowledge temporarily slaked, the boys turned to the gramophone. Among the records was one with the title, "Hail! smiling morn!", a piece traditionally played by brass bands in the West Riding on Christmas Day. Although the words contained not the least allusion to the festival, it spelt "Christmas" in Grannie's household as surely as did "O come, all ye faithful", and was absolutely taboo except in the immediate Christmas season.

When the situation was explained to him, the school friend promptly challenged Dick to play the record. Dick could never resist a dare, as well he knew: no matter how terrible the ensuing punishment, it was preferable to being branded a coward. He wound up the gramophone, put on the record and, while Margie held her breath in terror, the rousing strains of a brass band filled the summer air.

But only for a moment. No sooner had its opening chords rent the stillness than Nemesis could be heard running hotfoot up the flight of wooden stairs from the kitchen. Mother, the bearer of Grannie's wrath, snatched off the record like some avenging fury. Grannie was greatly displeased, nay, almost distraught; all manner of retribution was to be expected from the Almighty as a result of this sacrilege; the visitor was packed off home and the gramophone put away; and Dick, who had assuredly brought seven years' bad luck on the entire household, was sent to bed in disgrace.

Fishing was the "in" thing during the holidays. Children of all ages would flock to the park lake, each one clutching a small fishing net and a jamjar suspended from a loop of string. Dick kept one particularly rich haul of tiddlers and bloodsuckers in an old zinc bath in the back yard, feeding them on ants' eggs from the pet shop and simulating their natural habitat with a selection of stones, moss and weeds. The fish were removed for inspection so often that they soon died, probably from shock.

A similar fate awaited his goldfish which spent their brief lives swimming round and round a much too small glass bowl that stood on the mantelpiece in the back room. There was great excitement when the water had to be changed but it proved too much for the fish and inevitably the day came when first one and then the other was discovered floating, belly uppermost, among the ants' eggs on top of the water.

One summer the magic word current in the household was "Pinewood". To judge from Dick's raptures the place was synonomous with heaven. A large house on the edge of the Brontë country, it had been used as an army camp during the 1914-18 war and was later converted into a holiday camp by the enterprising Corporation which ran everything in the City of Bradford. On payment of a modest sum, parties of children from the city's schools could go there for a week to be refreshed by moorland air, good food and healthy exercise before returning to the smog and grime among which they had been reared.

Once it had been decided that Dick should join the fortunate party from Drummond Road Boys' School, Pinewood became the only topic of conversation, and everything revolved round his departure for that abode of the blest. The fact that the visit was to take place during term-time simply increased its desirability.

Alas, reality fell far short of the dream and he came home at the end of the week, unenthusiastic about the food and exhausted by the long tramps across the moors.

But for years the word, "Pinewood", conjured up in Margie's mind an ecstatic memory of the day she, too, had in person paid a visit to that idyllic spot. On the Tuesday afternoon parents had been allowed to visit their off-spring and see for themselves the delights of the venue. Dad couldn't be spared from the shop but Auntie Annie took a half-day off work, and she and Margie accompanied Mother.

The crowd which had gathered outside the school couldn't be squeezed into the waiting large blue open "sharrabang", ostentatiously named after Princess Mary. A second, equally large, bright yellow sharra was also filled. Still Mother, Auntie and Margie, not the pushing sort, stood hopefully on the causeway in the thinning crowd. To a flurry of waving and cheering, Princess Mary and her chubby yellow companion roared off in a cloud of dust and exhaust fumes.

At length a small, insignficant green sharra drew up and took the stragglers on board. Last to set out, they were not last to reach the promised land; they had the satisfaction en route of raising three ironic cheers as they chugged past Princess Mary, halted ignominiously by the roadside with a puncture.

Never before had Margie been away from her native city. To her surprise there were no mill chimneys or snickets to be seen in the prestigious town of Harrogate. The wide streets were lined with trees and there were even baskets of red and blue flowers hanging from the lamp standards. The sum streamed into the gracious panelled dining room at Pinewood where the air was odorous with the fragrance of boiled ham. The journey home through the drowsy, scented summer twilight, in the roomy back seat of the open shara, was sheer esctasy. Wonderful, glorious Pinewood!

No-one is quite such a god as an elder brother and Margie took for granted Dick's superiority in every field of endeavour. He had quitted the infants' department by the time she started school. When she reached the main school (seven to fourteen save for the fortunate minority who qualified at ten or eleven and left for a secondary school) he was in all the excitement of the scholarship year and became the first member of the family to embark on secondary education.

Though the boys' and girls' schools shared the same building in Drummond Road, the sexes were strictly segregated after the mixed infants' stage. There were separate entrances and playgrounds, and the establishments were cut off from each other by a ceiling-high partition dividing the two main halls.

Margie tried hard to keep up with her brother but a three-year gap is insuperable at that stage. A year after she moved up from the infants' to the "big" school, Dick, scholarship hurdle safely cleared, swept on to the glories of the Belle Vue Secondary School for Boys.

This educational advance entitled him immediately to longer holidays. He now had six whole weeks in the summer instead of a paltry month and a day, and could boast also of an extra week at Easter and three weeks instead of two at Christmas. The only time Margie scored was at Whitsuntide when the elementary schools had the traditional extra day tacked on to their week. It was small consolation.

Becoming one of the "Belle Vue bulldogs", as they were known to other (and lesser) schools, entitled Dick also to the glory of a navy school cap with band, button and badge in his house colours (green for House B) and a matching blazer with the school crest resplendent on the pocket.

With the exception of the Bradford Grammar School, which was independent of the local authority and took only fee-paying pupils, Belle Vue was regarded as **the** school in Bradford. In the words of a famous "old boy", J. B. Priestley, it was at the time "a-glitter with cups and shields". Its athletes were enjoying an unprecedented run of success and had won the city's Inter-School Sports no fewer than fourteen times; its soccer teams, too, in the claret and amber favoured also by Bradford City, had been gaining laurels; and its orchestra had returned once again flushed with success from the Wharfedale Festivals.

Dick's activities and conversation assumed a matching aura of glory. Cats became "moggies", tea was "char" and bread "Uncle Ned". He referred disparagingly to his sister as "Madge". His favourite epithets were "bally" and "ripping", his pet exclamation, "My only sainted aunt!" and his heroes Jack Dempsey and Gene Tunney. He talked casually about prefects and house meetings and something called a "bun fight", a rather unpleasant kind of Christmas party (Margie privately thought).

Dick's scientific knowledge was now such that he confidently predicted the imminent crashing to earth of the planet, Venus, though

46

perhaps the yarn owed more to the science fiction printed in the Boys' Magazine than to the staff at Belle Vue. On being told that Venus was a very big star, Margie began to experience a recurring nightmare in which she was trying in vain to clamber home from school down a back street completely blocked by large, flat, jagged pieces of broken star.

Dick also became acquainted with the activities of persons as diverse as Lars Porsena of Clusium and Bonnie Prince Charlie. He had already started French and in his second year took up German in preference to Latin. From then on his singing round the house was diversified by "Alle fische swimmen" as well as the better-known "Frère Jacques".

He seemed to be on familiar terms with members of the staff. English was taught by "Dolly" Dixon, History and Geography by "Molly" Morgan and French by "Mad Alice", known thus throughout the school on account of her scathing tongue.

Mr. Patrick, stout and short-tempered, ruled in "top school" where the youngest boys had most of their lessons. Once when he asked a boy why he wasn't getting on with his work, the excuse came in a particularly thick local accent: "Please, sir, there's no ink in t'inkwell."

According to Dick, the master's incredulous horror at this Philistinism was such that he foamed at the mouth.

"Tinkwell!" he thundered. "And **what** might a **tinkwell** be?"

"Elky" Clark ruled in the Art room. His method of persuading a boy to draw a reasonably accurate ellipse must surely have been unique. Standing behind him, stick poised at the ready over the victim's wavering knuckles, he would intone over and over again the magic phrase:

"Round and round and round we go,
And when we think we can, WE DO IT!"

The general strike started on 3 May, 1936, in Dick's second year at Belle Vue. He would come home each day and recount thrilling yarns of the exploits of members of staff, some of whom had managed to reach school from the wilds of Ilkley or Bingley on rickety borrowed cycles or the pillion of a temperamental motorbike. The rights and wrongs of the strike were never discussed: the over-riding obsession seemed to be getting to work by hook or by crook.

The one field in which Dick distinguished himself at Belle Vue was swimming. In spite of the disadvantage of being physically a late developer and therefore not very tall for his age, he was good enough to represent his school each year at the boys' Inter-School Swimming Gala.

This was an occasion the family never missed. Filled with pride in the results of his coaching, Dad never grudged paying for the best seats on the edge of the swimming bath, where spectators were issued with towels to protect them against splashing. As the five secondary schools fought out the issue, the excitement rose to fever pitch and the clamour grew deafening. Dick never won a race but he was often commended in the diving.

Chapter Eight

Auntie

The French would have called Auntie Annie "une joile laide". She was less than five feet tall, with dark hair, a turned-up nose and merry brown eyes.

An accident at the age of two had changed the course of her life. Sitting on a wall, watching the older children playing, she had over-balanced and fallen backwards into the field far below. It was some time before Grannie noticed the lump on her spine.

Grandad, always concerned about the welfare of his children, took her straight to the doctor. But it seemed that nothing could be done. Even the drastic remedy suggested ... lying strapped to a board for several years ... was not put forward as a certain cure and might well have proved useless. More specialised medical advice was out of the question as, with nine children to provide for, Grandad had no money to spare for consultants' fees.

Outwardly Auntie accepted her twisted spine and stunted figure with an uncomplaining cheerfulness. When the pain in her back was bad, she took an evil-smelling hot drink of valerian and skullcap, a remedy obtained from the herbalist up the road.

Mother never went back on the promise she had made Grandad, that Auntie would always find a home with her. Apart from one twelve-month period, Auntie spent the rest of her life with Mother and Dad and their children. In spite of obvious drawbacks the arrangement worked suprisingly well.

Auntie lavished on her sister's children all the affection she would have bestowed on a family of her own. She loved them all but Dick was her special favourite and in her eyes he could do no wrong.

Auntie had been apprenticed to a local private dressmaker and worked for her for many years. Mrs. Foulds's "haute couture" business was run from her own home in the best part of the city. The road where she lived boasted a much-prized expanse of dusty grass, trees and shrubs known as the boulevard, where the residents exercised their dogs and sent their children out to play.

The workroom was a chilly attic with a linoleum-covered floor and a dormer window too high to see out of except by standing on a chair.

When Mrs. Foulds's clientèle (whom Mother referred to as "the upper ten") came for fittings they were received in the comfortable ground floor sitting room which boasted a luxurious Chesterfield suite.

Mrs. Foulds had known the family for years and took a great interest in the children. Dick and Margie were once invited for tea, an uncomfortable occasion in the course of which they grew hot with embarrassment at having to carry out under her eagle eye their clumsy assault on boiled eggs, a delicacy seldom encountered at home. Margie was more afraid of the gracious but steely lady with the silver hair and superior voice than she was of another member of the household, the huge Alsatian dog whose size belied his gentleness.

In spite of her disconcerting manner Mrs. Foulds often unbent sufficiently to confide in Annie, as she always called her senior employee, some highly confidential and sometimes even scandalous stories about her clients.

It was imperative, for example, that fitting appointments for two middle-aged customers be arranged so that they never met. For was it not rumoured on impeccable authority that, much to his wife's chagrin, Mr. A. was having an affaire with Mrs. B., their widowed neighbour?

The Gilbertian liaison engineered between the gauche new curate and the decidedly plain and no longer youthful daughter of one of the pillars of the church formed another talking point. All the harmless cleric had done, apparently, after his introduction by the vicar, was pay a second call on the family: he was pounced on then and there by the predatory mama and commanded to declare his intentions. The hapless youth was either too bewildered or too timid to protest his disinterest and soon, although in private Mrs. Foulds expressed her disgust at her client's contemptible behaviour, the workroom was a-flurry with the wedding order.

Auntie might be the charge hand but Mrs. Foulds was the boss. Her only child, a sweet-natured girl with no trace of her mother's domineering personality, worked happily among the apprentices. Although very much under her mother's thumb, she joined with enthusiasm in all the frolics that went on when Mrs. Foulds was busy downstairs with a client.

A good deal of harmless teasing and fun helped to pass the hours of the long day which stretched, with a short break for a sandwich lunch, from eight thirty to half past five or even six.

Most of the hands were apprentices in their teens ... "flappers", in the slang of the twenties. As soon as Mrs. Foulds was safely out of earshot the bolder spirits would break into one of the hit songs of the moment or even start demonstrating the Charleston or Black Bottom, fancy garters daringly revealed as short skirts swung in time to the syncopated rhythm.

Many popular songs high-lighted the wedding day, life's supreme event to which they were all looking forward with an anticipation faintly tinged with apprehension.

> "How do you feel when you've married your ideal?
> Ever so goosey, goosey, goosey, goosey!
> How do you feel when the parson's on the kneel?
> Ever so goosey, goosey, goosey, goosey!
> Walking down the aisle in a kind of daze,
> Do you get the wind up when the organ plays?
> How do you feel when the bells begin to peal?
> Ever so goosey, goosey, goosey, goosey!"

The comic element predominated in many of them.

> "Mary Ellen at the church turned up,
> Her Ma turned up and her Pa turned up.
> Her sister Gert, her rich Uncle Bert
> And the parson in his long white shirt turned up.
> BUT ...
> No bridegroom with the ring turned up,
> Just a telegram boy with his nose turned up.
> The telegram said he didn't want to wed
> And they'd find him in the river with his toes turned up!"

Not all the top tunes had a comedy theme for the twenties were the heyday of Valentino. His romantic image inspired daring songs like "The Sheikh of Araby", the words of which set every flapper's heart pounding.

> "I'm the Sheikh of Araby; your love belongs to me.
> At night when you're asleep, into your tent I'll creep.
> The stars that shine above will light our way to love.
> You're all the world to me, the Sheikh of Araby."

Alas! there was a chronic shortage of men in the aftermath of World War One so most of the girls had to content themselves with the vicarious pleasure of sewing someone else's bridal gown. Overtime was obligatory when there was a wedding order on hand. The bride

51

invariably came from a well-to-do family so there were several bridesmaids' dresses and perhaps even a pageboy's satin suit to make as well.

As a special treat Margie was once allowed into the workroom among the shrouded rows of slipper satin, ninon and georgette evening gowns to see the bridal dress for an important wedding. Layer upon layer of tissue paper was removed to reveal a fairy-tale gown of white crepe de Chine with a long train lined in palest pink. The intricate embroidery, appliquéd lovers' knots and shell-stitched edging on the train were all Auntie's work.

Auntie's favourite was the popular romantic classic from which Margie's hated pet name was derived.

"Margie! I'm always thinking of you,
Margie! I'll tell the world I love you.
Don't forget your promise to me!
I have bought the
Home and ring and
Everything for
Margie! You've been my inspiration;
Days are never blue.
After all is said and done
There is really only one:
Oh, Margie, Margie, it's you!''

Auntie was more interested in her nieces' clothes than her own: she made all their frocks and some of their coats. Even children's dresses featured the dropped waistline and diminutive skirt characteristic of the twenties.

The milliner up the road turned a couple of remnants from Mrs. Foulds's workroom into a magnificent best hat for Margie. It was of blue crepe de Chine with a brim lined in flowered silk. A wide swathe of the crepe de Chine swept round the crown and cascaded in dangling ends half a yard long. It created a sensation in Sunday School.

Margie took a lively interest in the fashion magazines Auntie consulted when she was sewing at home. She would beg for an old one and make paper dolls by cutting out the elegant ladies who filled its pages. The only thing that pleased her more was a paper doll bought specially from the stationer's, with a complete wardrobe of paper dresses, coats and hats. Each garment could be secured to the doll's shoulders by means of tabs, while a convenient slit in the hats allowed them to slide neatly on to her head. The promise of a "real paper doll" would even get Margie to the dentist's for the removal of a troublesome milk tooth.

Auntie was on visiting terms with several of the girls from the workroom and sometimes took Margie with her. Snapshots of one dashing pair, Winnie Rollings and her sister, Myra, taken on holiday in Bournemouth, showed them sporting the very latest craze, beach pyjamas.

Tennis was all the rage. Sometimes on a Saturday afternoon Mother, Auntie and Margie, with Baby in the pram, would watch the glamorous sisters emerging with their boy friends for a game on the public courts in the park.

Margie was so much impressed with their short white dresses, ankle socks and Lenglen bandeaux and their partners' white shirts, immaculate white flannels and Blanco-ed pumps that she made tennis outfits for her paper dolls.

Auntie fulfilled one of the children's dearest wishes the day she took them for a sail on the pleasure boat which operated on Manningham park lake during the summer. The newly acquired motor launch, its smart red awning and Union Jack flapping in the breeze, had been named "The Princess Mary" in honour of that royal lady's recent marriage. Anticipation was, as usual, more pleasurable than reality. The small craft was uncomfortably crowded and the chilly trip ended in disaster for Margie, who managed to lose one of her gloves overboard. It was Auntie who took Margie along to the park to see that popular and romantic figure, the Prince of Wales, when he paid a brief visit to the city. Incidentally, a year or two later when a member of the royal family, the dowager Queen Alexandra, died, all the newspapers came out on the day of the funeral with pages bordered in black as a token of mourning, and the schools were closed for half a day.

Margie's first visit to the theatre was arranged and paid for by Auntie who took her, at the age of six, to see the pantomime, "Red Riding Hood", at the Prince's. She sat spellbound through a glittering, bowdlerised version of the Grimm brothers' crude classic, enchanted by the gaiety of the nubile chorus and the ethereal dancing of the fairy queen.

The comedians were tedious and their jokes incomprehensible: they merely interrupted the story. But Margie's attention was riveted when Red Riding Hood started singing "Whisp'ring", one of the hit songs of the day, to her handsome prince, resplendent in velvet cloak, sequinned tunic and shoes with high heels such as even Sunshine Susie of "The Rainbow" never wore. Margie was enthralled in spite of the unsuitability of the musical repertoire. For why, argued her logical mind, should two people who had only just met each other in the forest start singing:

"Drift with me
Along the shores of Minnetonka
Where I first made love to you!
Every tree
Along the shores of Minnetonka
Seems to whisper, 'Love, I'm blue!'
Come to me,
My love, and hum to me
That dreamy melody
You sang that night you said you'd always
Drift with me
Along the shores of Minnetonka
Where I first made love to you!"

Grandmother's cottage in the forest was furnished with an outsize window through which everything that happened inside could clearly been seen. Nobody was eaten up, of course, not even grandmother, but Margie was so terrified of the wolf that she crawled under her seat in the front row of the dress circle. She was coaxed from her hiding place only just in time to see Red Riding Hood (who had exchanged her scarlet cloak, black pumps and prim white apron for a shimmering bridal gown that eclipsed any in Mrs. Foulds's workroom) united with a befeathered and bejewelled prince to the vociferous satisfaction of the entire company.

Next year the tension again became well-nigh unbearable as, during the matinée interval, Dick Whittington's man-sized cat attempted the perilous climb from the stage right up to the dress circle, where he calmly proceeded to drink tea from the cups of the astonished patrons.

Auntie was godmother to her sister's three children. She took her duties seriously and one or other of them usually accompanied her on a Sunday night to evensong at St. Luke's church across the road. Margie didn't exactly enjoy the experience though it provided an interesting change from staying at home. Even on summer evenings

54

only a dim, religious light filtered through the stained glass windows, in keeping with the solemnity of the occasion.

In spite of her sincerely held Christian convictions, Auntie was just as superstitious as Grannie. She never walked under ladders and always threw spilt salt over her left shoulder with her right hand. She tried to remember to say, "White rabbits!" three times on the first day of the month before uttering another syllable; doing this was so lucky that you might receive a present during the month, whether it was your birthday or not.

Besides a copy of Old Moore's Almanack (which Grannie insisted on buying and reading every New Year, though its dire prognostications were fortunately seldom fulfilled) the family also possessed a Dream Book with a lurid purple cover. You looked up the subject matter of your dream in the flimsy paperback as in a dictionary, to find what it might portend.

Auntie was a firm believer and consulted the book regularly, hoping, perhaps, for some miracle to soften the harsh blow dealt her by fate. The miracle was to be found in her cheerful, unselfish personality.

Chapter Nine

Georgie

If Dick was Auntie's favourite, then Margie was Uncle George's. **She** was certainly very fond of **him**. In the dark winter days when the schools' normal two-hour dinner break was reduced to an hour and a half (so that they could finish in daylight at four o'clock instead of in darkness at the usual time of four-thirty), he was usually going back to work just as she was setting off for the afternoon session. Nothing suited her better than dancing down the street, holding his hand and chattering, as he would tell her Mother afterwards, fifty to the dozen.

It didn't matter that he smelled of the thick twist he "smooked" in his pipe, nor that at least one day's growth of beard was sprouting on his chin, nor that he was wearing a threadbare old jacket and collarless striped union shirt with no tie. He was "Georgie", her friend and ally, always sympathetic and appreciative.

"My! yon's a real bobby-dazzler!" he'd exclaim whenever she flaunted her latest bit of finery.

The middle-aged bachelor was very fond of his sister's children. During the war, when he was working on munitions and Mother had only a private's meagre pay coming in, he often spent his money on fruit for them, although the price of even one apple or orange was outrageous.

Georgie was the third of Grannie's sons. He was several years older than Mother but not unlike her in appearance with the same black curly hair. He had considerable intelligence and often tried to help Dick when he got stuck with his Maths homework, but Geometry and Algebra were beyond the scope of his limited education.

Georgie relished spicy food. He would often come in after the children's teatime with something tasty like a pair of kippers or bloaters for his own meal. The smell of them grilling on the grid-iron in front of the kitchen fire was so appetising that they couldn't help begging for a taste. Alas! Margie could never cope with the bones, and invariably got one stuck in her throat. She fared better with the Gorgonzola cheese to which she and Georgie were both partial, though she couldn't stomach the raw onion he habitually ate with it.

The children believed implicitly in Georgie's anecdotes in spite of the openly sceptical attitude of the rest of the family.

"He's having you on!" they would laugh when he started, usually in the middle of Sunday dinner.

"When a new king comes to t'throne," he would yarn, "'e hes a lot o' royal banquets at Buckin'ham Palace an' ivverybody gets invited. It's a rare do, wi' mebbe a dozen different courses, an' flunkeys in livery waitin' at t' table."

"T' time I wor theer," he went on, warming to his subject as the children's eyes grew rounder, "ther' wor an owd chap sat next ter me. We wor 'evin' rabbit pie," he would add, glancing at his plate, "an', by gum! 'e **wor** enjoyin' it! 'E wor a bit slow, like ... left 'is teeth at 'ome, I shouldn't wonder! ... an' afore 'e'd 'awf finished, t' flunkey tried ter snatch t' plate away an' give 'im t' next course. But t' owd chap worn't 'evin' ony o' that, an' kept tight ho'd o' it. 'Nay, lad,' 'e says ter t' flunkey, 'tha'll he' ter wait till Ah've finished this 'ere rabbit pie: it's champion!' and, Georgie concluded, "t' king roared wi' laughin'.'"

Another of his stories probably **did** have a grain of truth it it.

It was Georgie who got up to light the kitchen fire every morning. He would prop the blawjohn in front of it to create a draught and then, when the fire was drawing nicely, he'd take a quick look round for any blackclocks that hadn't scurried off fast enough to their holes behind the skirting board when he lit the gas.

A friend of his, he said, arrived home late one night when the fire was out and everybody had gone to bed. The minute he lit the gas mantle he could see that the kitchen floor was solid with blackclocks: you couldn't put a foot between them. It was too good an opportunity to miss so, quick as a flash, he measured his length on the ground so as to kill as many as possible. He said he could hear their shells cracking under him.

Like most of his brothers, Georgie had served his apprenticeship as a cabinet maker. His boss, generally referred to by Mother as "that skinflint, Clayton", wasn't noted for fair treatment of his employees and Georgie was often on short time. Times were bad for skilled craftsmen and there was little chance of moving to other employment.

Georgie's hobby was repairing watches. He would sit for hours at his workbench under the skylight in his attic bedroom, tweezers in hand, magnifying glass to his eye, fiddling patiently with the intricate movement of an old clock or watch that no professional would have bothered with. He did it for love rather than money and was delighted when he succeeded in getting a watch to go.

But best of all in the children's eyes, Georgie could make fireworks. For his speciality, **Mount Vesuvius,** he poured shiny grey powder into little cones of thick dark paper. They didn't produce the spectacular golden rain and coloured stars of a Roman candle but glowed with the soft pink and green of Bengal lights.

Georgie's allotment on Heaton Hill, a mile or so away, was a bit of a family joke as he didn't spend much time there. Sometimes he took the children with him and they would come back with a bunch of turnips or radishes and a cabbage or two.

On a hot summer day Georgie would take Dick and Margie into the herbalist's for a glass of sarsaparilla on their way home from the allotment. It was a gloomy shop with a strange musty smell. Behind the mahogany counter were rows and rows of little drawers labelled with queer names; above them the large glass bottles with stoppers were full of dried pods and dirty-looking powders, not sweets. But the sarsaparilla, which flowed from the tap of a large wooden barrel, had a lovely refreshing tang.

Unfortunately Georgie was fond of something more potent than sarsaparilla and spent most evenings at the public house, usually returning home after the family had gone to bed.

Every Monday dinnertime he handed Margie a song-sheet on which were printed the words of the latest hits. She already had a good idea how some of them went, as the boys in the street were never tired of yelling snatches of such popular ditties as "Eat more fruit!", "Horsey, keep your tail up!", "Yes! we have no bananas" and "When it's night-time in Italy, it's Wednesday over here."

They had their own version of some special favourites. Instead of
"How in the world
Can the old folks tell
That it ain't gonna rain no more?",
they would bawl joyfully,
"How in the heck
Can a feller wash his neck
If it ain't gonna rain no more?"

Margie was delighted with Georgie's song-sheets because, besides the full version of comedy songs like "All by yourself in the moonlight"

58

and "The more we are together", they also contained the words of the romantic ballads she much preferred: "Romany Rose", "Peggy O'Neil" and "There's a blue ridge round my heart, Virginia."

She could never understand why Mother didn't like Georgie giving her the song-sheets. What she didn't realise, of course, was that they had been handed round in the pub the previous Saturday and Sunday evenings. Although Dad wasn't a teetoller, he didn't frequent public houses and thought Georgie went there much too often.

Late one Christmas Eve the family was roused by someone shouting and hammering on the seldom-used front door. The children, waking in their parents' bedroom, became aware also of an altercation going on between Mother and Dad. The shouting and hammering grew more and more vehement and at last not only Dad and Mother but, it seemed, the entire household, except for themselves, clambered out of bed and went down to investigate.

In the commotion that ensued the children could distinguish, against a background of confusion, the sound of heavy footsteps accompanied by strange bursts of laughter and loud snatches of song. At the same time other voices could be heard shushing and remonstrating and pleading for quiet. The babel rolled past their bedroom door and up the wooden steps to the attic and Dad and Mother came back at last into the dark bedroom.

"Who was it? Father Christmas?" the children asked eagerly.

But Mother was in no mood for answering questions. In fact, considering that it was Christmas Eve, she was very short-tempered. She told them in a cross voice to mind their own business and get to sleep.

It was several days before Margie found out from Dick the cause of all the commotion. Georgie had been celebrating Christmas so well that a friend had had to escort him home and rouse the household, and it had taken the combined efforts of the family to get him up to bed.

Chapter Ten

Auntie Em

Mother's youngest sister was the family pianist. She seldom performed but, on the rare occasions when she was in the mood, Margie would listen spellbound to the rippling stream of arpeggios that cascaded from her fingers.

But by the time Margie was considered old enough to learn to play, Auntie Em had mysteriously disappeared, never to return. Miss Hodgson, a young colleague of Auntie Annie's, who had no qualifications as a music teacher, started giving her lessons at nine-pence a time.

Locked in the unheated front room every day for a half-hour that seemed an eternity, Margie soon wearied of her struggles with "Lightly Row" and "The Blue Bells of Scotland". As the pieces in the Ideal Tutor Book grew progressively more unmanageable for her small, cold, fumbling hands, she would turn her attention increasingly from "Stephanie Gavotte" and "Blumenlied" to the much more interesting books of music which her aunt had left behind.

Auntie Em had been a bookbinder by profession and the large black-bound volumes with gold lettering on the front were samples of her work. They contained songs rather than pieces. As Margie had a good ear and, in any case, had heard her aunt sing many of them before, she soon became absorbed in picking out with one finger the tunes of such well-known ballads as "Come back to Erin", "Alice where art thou?", "Kathleen Mavoureen" and "Killarney".

But in one or two the cosy Victorians had indulged an unexpected penchant for the macabre. The words of "The diver", especially, sent a chill to the heart and Margie would turn the page hastily before his horrific figure could take shape in her vivid imagination. Unfortunately the words imprinted themselves indelibly on her memory.

> "In the caverns deep of the ocean cold
> The diver is seeking a treasure of gold,
> Risking his life for the spoil of a wreck,
> Taking rich gems from the dead on her deck.
> How fearful the life of the diver must be,
> Walking alone, walking alone,
> Walking alone in the depths of the sea!"

Her favourite among Auntie Em's music books was the volume in which half a dozen popular songs of the immediate pre-war decade had been bound together. She couldn't decide which of these sentimental ballads she loved best: "When you come home, dear", "Old-fashioned town" or "Little grey home in the west".

Delicate sprays of palest pink roses adorned the title page of Carrie Jacobs-Bond's "Perfect Day". A shaggy pilgrim in a broad-brimmed hat, with a huge bundle on his back and a six-foot staff in his hand, was setting out on a long, long, zigzag trail a-winding beyond the pine trees and snow-capped peaks of another cover page, to the land of his dreams. The minutes of her practice half-hour ticked away as Margie puzzled over the meaning of "amour" and "Je t'aime", for the words of "Just a little love, a little kiss" were written in French as well as English.

Trouble flared up between the sisters the winter after Grandad died. Margie had just come in from school and was thawing her frozen hands in a bowl of hot water at the slopstone. Mother and Grannie were folding sheets and putting them through the mangle to save ironing. The quarrel that erupted between Auntie Em and Mother was so violent that they almost came to blows. When Grannie tried to intervene, Mother turned on her, scarlet-faced and furious, and said that, of course, she always took Emily's part.

Meanwhile Margie and three-year-old Baby stood aghast at the unusual spectacle of Grannie extremely upset and Mother on the verge of tears. Mother managed to pull herself together sufficiently to whisk the two children off for their dinner. But not long after that, Auntie Em went away. There was no Grandad to fetch her back and the family never saw her again.

Chapter Eleven

Mixed Infants

Margie went to school at the statutory age of five. An earlier start was not prohibited: some children attended from three years old. Jack Ambler, the boy across the back street, who was several months younger than Margie, had been going for some time and was quite blasé about it.

On the first morning she was very apprehensive but, with true Yorkshire grit, made no fuss when Mother returned home. As Jack was the only child she knew in the class, she was allowed for the first day to sit among the boys, between him and a pleasant lad called Alfred. Normally the sexes were strictly segregated, boys sitting at one side of the classroom and girls the other.

Trouble arose at playtime when Margie followed Jack and Alfred into the playground. They went straight to the boys' urinals. As small boys quite often relieved themselves in public, she was, fortunately, only mildly startled at the sight that met her gaze before she was seized by authority and whisked off to more suitable regions.

Playtime over, the class was sent into the main hall for a singing lesson with Miss Dobson, the head teacher. Jack and Alfred, with Margie in tow, made at once for the far end of the room where there were a few desks with attached forms.

"These are for the grunters," they explained. "**We're** grunters! It's more fun being a grunter. You can crayon instead of having to sing. **You'd** better be a grunter as well."

Margie had no idea what a grunter was but she sat down obediently, picked up a crayon and began, without much confidence, to draw on the paper provided. Drawing wasn't her strong point. As the lively strains of "The cuckoo is a pretty bird" carried down the hall, she wondered whether, in agreeing to become a grunter, she had chosen the better part.

Her sojourn among the species was short-lived. A few lessons later the head teacher, observing that the ranks of her choir were dwindling in inverse proportion to the growing company of grunters, made a lightning raid on their haven and bore several off in triumph.

A bewildered Margie found herself in the middle of the choir facing

Miss Dobson. Perched dangerously on a chair and brandishing a stick in maniacal fashion, the head teacher proceeded to bellow instructions as they sang. Terrified, Margie obediently opened her mouth wide and began to utter something about the cuckoo, though she'd never before heard of one and didn't know the words. Later, when she had become more familiar with them, she thought them excessively stupid.

"The cuckoo is a pretty bird:
She singeth as she flies.
She bringeth us good tidings:
She telleth us no lies.
She sucketh all sweet flowers
To keep her throttle clear,
And every time she singeth,
    'Cuckoo! cuckoo!'
The summer draweth near.

"The cuckoo is a witty bird:
No other nest hath she.
She flits across the meadow:
She sings in every tree.
She flies th' approaching winter:
She hates the rain and snow.
Like her I would be singing,
    'Cuckoo! cuckoo!'
And off with her I'd go."

By the quickest route, which zigzagged across several roads by way of a couple of narrow snickets, school was a ten-minute walk away. Leaving home soon after the mill buzzer had sounded half-past eight, you could be walking along Drummond Road as the "early bell" was clanging at a quarter to nine.

But there was often a good reason for delay. The scarlet fever van might be drawn up outside one of the terraced houses en route. A morbidly curious crowd would stand watching at a safe distance as a bundle wrapped in a red blanket was carried out on a stretcher and driven off in the ambulance to the children's hospital nearby. If "scarlet fever" was a dreaded name, the word to strike real terror to the heart in those days before immunisation was "diphtheria", as the illness claimed many a child victim.

On one memorable occasion a funeral procession was drawn up outside a house in Drummond Road just as the children were returning for the afternoon session. Each of the sombre cabs, draped in black, had its complement of white-faced mourners and was drawn by two sable horses. As the drivers, sitting high in front, muffled in rugs and wearing black top hats, cracked their whips and the long line of cabs and tossing black-plumed heads moved slowly away, an indelible picture of gloom must have been printed on many a childish mind.

The best walk home was on Friday afternoons but not just because school had finished for the week. The delicious smell of fresh bread was wafted through every open doorway as housewives, their weekly baking done, set to work fettling their front steps which were then edged with white or yellow donkey stone. In an orgy of cleanliness they would even wash the flags of the causeway opposite the door.

Mother was surprised when Miss Tatham told her that her quiet little girl had turned into a chatterbox. She had moved across the classroom and made friends with Gladys, a stolid, forthright child with red hair and freckles and no pretensions to good looks, and Cissie Goodchild, a pretty child with dark ringlets who lived up to her name.

What did they chatter about? Names and birthdays seemed all important. Lively Mary Greenwood claimed some sort of distinction because she had been born on St. Patrick's Day. Year after year as March 17th came round, Margie remembered, long after Mary's premature death, that it was her birthday.

One day the burning question was: "Are you a War Baby?" It was hardly surprising to discover that the description fitted every child in the class as they had all been born during the war.

Recollections of life in Miss Tatham's class were blurred and fragmentary. "Mashed Taters", as the boys privately called her, sometimes brought a cup of hot milk into the classroom at the end of afternoon playtime, and would sip it whilst reading the class a story. Delicately removing the skin which had formed on top, she would place it in the saucer while the children, who seldom got anything as nourishing to drink, watched, fascinated. Eight or more years were to elapse before authority came to realise that they, as well as their teachers, needed refreshment at school.

Discipline was upheld by the simple expedient of dragooning the class into various more or less uncomfortable sitting positions to prevent fidgeting. The number of misdemeanours a child could commit with arms folded or hands clasped on the desk was limited. Delinquency became virtually impossible even for the boys (the chief offenders)

Margie with decorated pram for May Day celebration

when the command changed to "Hands behind backs!" or, worse still, "Hands on heads!" The fatiguing business of keeping both hands on the head became positive torture after a very few minutes.

The zenith of achievement in the infants' school seemed to be the learning and reciting of the twice times table as far as "Twice ten are twenty". Margie was utterly amazed when Katie, who had several older brothers, informed her that twice eleven were twenty-two and twice twelve twenty-four. It was like discovering a new dimension.

Margie couldn't remember learning to read ... it just happened, though there was quite a bit of "The cat sat on the mat" to be got through first.

Occasionally the routine of life in the infants' school was broken for the observance of a festival. The only preparation for Christmas seemed to be the making of coloured paper lanterns. Each child was given a ruled sheet of paper from an ordinary exercise book and told to crayon it all over in any pattern or colour scheme. This presented difficulties as the nature of the end product was not divulged. The crayoned sheets were then folded across and cut into narrow strips, the sides and edges being left intact. With the addition of a paper loop and a lick of glue, they were magically transformed into Chinese lanterns to be strung decoratively across the main hall.

May Day, though not a holiday, was quite an occasion. Every infant was expected to take to school a toy decorated for the festival ... pram, tricycle, scooter, wheelbarrow or fairy cycle. Margie usually took her best doll, Brenda, resplendent in blue velvet cloak and hood, in the pram which Mother and Auntie painstakingly decked with rosettes and streamers of red, white and blue crepe paper.

Each class posed with its decorated toys for an official photograph, and parents were invited to watch the procession round the playground in the afternoon. Unfortunately Spring arrives late in the north of England and even when May Day wasn't actually wet, it was bitterly cold. Margie would be muffled up as for a polar expedition, coat, scarf, mittens and long woollen stockings incongruously teamed with sandals and a Panama hat.

The day of the medical inspection, though scarcely a festival, was a red letter day because Mother came to school for the occasion, bringing with her a paper bag full of pink and white sugared coconut chips. Recollections of the nurse's search for nits behind the ears and the shaming exposure of one's naked chest to the doctor's stethoscope were expunged by the delight of sharing one's favourite

66

sweets afterwards with special friends, whose number registered a sudden remarkable increase.

When Dick was subjected to a medical inspection in the infants' school, a few older girls were detailed to help the children dress again. Dick's helper was flummoxed by his leggings, which could best be described as knee-length spats with a strap under the instep and buttons and buttonholes all the way up the outer leg. Mother, coming to meet him after school, could hardly control her mirth at his comical appearance, for the leggings had been put on the wrong feet and were buttoned up the inside of the leg. Years afterwards she and Auntie, a couple of rare gigglers when in the mood, would be seized with a fit of hysterics at the recollection of Dick's shuffling progress home.

After the age of seven the sexes were totally segregated for the remainder of their school careers. It was only in the infants' playground that boys and girls were permitted to play together.

On the whole this was an amicable proceeding and children joined voluntarily in corporate games like "The big ship sailed through the Alli-alli-o on the twentieth of December." In this singing game a long line of children with hands clasped pressed through a series of arches made as each child and his neighbour held up their linked arms in turn, until a complete circle was achieved with all hands crossed as for "Auld Lang Syne". The final movement was the lightning unwinding of the long snake.

"The farmer wants a wife" was a favourite with the girls because of its matrimonial associations but the boys had to be cajoled into playing it. A boy was put in the middle and a ring of children with hands linked circled round him, singing,

> "The farmer wants a wife,
> The farmer wants a wife.
> Ee-ay-ee-ay,
> The farmer wants a wife."

A mate having been chosen by the embarrassed farmer and taken into the middle, the game continued with "The wife wants a child", "The child wants a nurse" and "The nurse wants a dog".

The role of dog was an unwanted honour for the game concluded, "We all pat the dog", with everybody taking part in the boisterous back-slapping to which the unlucky animal had to submit.

One quick-witted victim resisted the onslaught by hastily inventing an additional verse, "The dog wants a bone". This extricated him from his difficulties but the crowd was not to be cheated of its fun and gathered round this time to thump the unlucky "bone", chanting "We all pat the bone". That was how the game acquired a new and ridiculous conclusion.

Margie's favourite game was the traditional encounter between the Romans and the English. It was difficult to choose between the insolent, prestigious Romans and the equally arrogant but indigenous English, but patriotism usually asserted itself. Besides, the English undoubtedly had the best lines.

The confronting rows of opponents, arms linked, advanced menacingly in turn, singing their set piece.

Romans: "Have you any bread and wine?
           For we are the Romans!
           Have you any bread and wine?
           For we are the Roman soldiers!"

English: "Yes, we have some bread and wine,
           For we are the English!
           Yes, we have some bread and wine,
           For we are the English soldiers!"

Romans: "Then we will have **one** cup full," etc.

English: "No, you won't have **one** cup full," etc.

Romans: "Then we will have **two** cups full."

English: "No, you won't have **two** cups full."

Romans: "Then we will have **three** cups full."

English: "No, you won't have **three** cups full."

Romans (advancing with appropriate clawing actions):
           "Then we'll send our cats to scratch."

English (in lordly fashion):
           "We don't care for the cats or you."

Romans (getting desperate):
           "Then we'll send our dogs to bite."

English: "We don't care for the dogs or you."

Romans: "Then we'll tell our king of you." (rather feeble, this!)'

English (triumphantly):
           "We don't care for the king or you."

This was too much. Obviously only one course of action was left.

Romans: "Are you ready for a fight?" etc.

English: "Yes, we're ready for a fight!" etc.

At this point the opposing ranks would break up for individual combat and, to satisfy the boys, there had to be some sort of encounter. Scuffling over, the protagonists would form one large circle and hop or limp round in common affliction, matching their simulated disability to the words of the remaining verses.

All: "Now we've only got one arm,
leg,
eye,
ear,
anything else you could think of,
For we are the Romans,
English," etc.

Margie was always thrilled by this rousing game though its excellent moral ... the futility of war ... no doubt passed her by. The companions with whom she played it at Drummond Road Infants' School, many of them fatherless as a result of the 1914-18 war, had barely reached their twenties when they were sucked into the maw of World War Two.

Chapter Twelve

The Back Street

Life surged through the back street: it was considered swanky to use one's front door except on special occasions.

Tradesmen always came the back way. Every morning the horse-drawn milk-float rumbled slowly over the cobbles with its load of clanking churns. The milkman carried a smaller oval container to the back door. Using a pint-sized metal dipper he would dispense the milk into the householder's own jugs. He always plunged the dipper back into the churn and added a little extra to make sure of giving good measure.

The greengrocer and coalman hollered their wares as their horses and carts clattered along. So did Salt Jim, a queer character whose handcart was laden with blocks of salt. The "yest" man rang a bell: he came twice a week for nearly every housewife baked her own bread. An occasional visitor was the rag and bone man whose string of shiny balloons danced above his cart in obscene contrast to its pile of dingy cast-offs.

The rare visits of the tingalari always drew a crowd of children, fascinated by the chattering, red-coated monkey chained to the top of the instrument. Adults would lurk in doorways or peer from behind lace curtains, eager to enjoy the gaiety of the harsh, mechanical music but unwilling to thoil a precious copper for the Italian musician.

At dusk the lamplighter started on his round, kindling the gaslights to a mellow glow with the magic rod he carried. He was followed by the paper boy bawling his unintelligible "Latest City sha-a-ame!" Margie knew that the city was the town centre for it said "City" on all the tramcars going that way. But what scandal erupted there daily, to be blazoned each evening in the pages of the **Telegraph and Argus**? It was years before the meaning of his raucous shout, "Latest editi...on!" dawned on her.

But the life which surged most fiercely through the back street was that of the children. There they rolled their marbles, whipped their tops and climbed other people's garden walls. In fine weather the street was not only their communal playground but often their battlefield.

One house down the street was used as an orphanage. The seven or eight girls who lived there were never allowed out to play for when they weren't at school they had all the housework to do. Their faces were raw with cleanliness and their bodies permanently swathed in voluminous pinafores and long black stockings and boots. A perpetual banging of brooms and shaking of mats mingled with the scoldings of the matron as she dragooned her charges without any trace of affection. Mother said it was no way to bring children up.

Beyond the orphanage lived the Harrops. Their brood of five consisted of the twins, plump Flossie and scraney Joey, who were too young for school; Stan, a pleasant lad about Margie's age; know-all Lizzie who was eighteen months Margie's senior; and the eldest, Bert, the same age as Dick.

Jack Ambler's house was in adjoining Athol Road but his back gate was directly opposite Margie's. He was a good-looking boy, an only child, the pride of his parents. His father suffered from some disability as a result of the war and seemed to be permanently under the weather.

The Warburtons lived further along Athol Road but their two boys, Derek and Paul, who were about the same age as Dick and Margie, were hardly ever allowed out to play. Their father, well-known on the stage, was seldom at home and their mother seemed more concerned about her pet Pomeranian than her sons. Mrs. Warburton was totally different from every other mother in the street. Tall and very stylish, with high heels, a Marcel wave and a great deal of make-up, she exemplified the popular image of the flapper.

Mother disapproved of her on the quiet and felt sorry for her boys. She often went out, leaving them locked in the house. They got into mischief and on her return she would give them a good hiding. Her shouts and their yells and screams could be heard half-way down the street. Yet on the rare occasions when she stopped to speak, in a cultured voice with no trace of the prevailing northern accent, she was perfectly charming.

There were no girls of Margie's age in the back street so she played with the boys. They tolerated a girl in their midst surprisingly well.

Margie was genuinely fond of them and put up with their uncouth habits which included scribbling unintelligible four-letter words on walls and occasionally urinating in public.

One thing she never became reconciled to was their passion for bombs. These could be bought from any sweet shop or newsagent's and made a satisfying substitute for fireworks during eleven months of the year. A tiny paper cap was inserted between two small grooved hemispheres made of solid lead. These were then tied together on the end of a length of string. When the primed "bomb" was smacked on the ground, preferably behind the back of an unsuspecting victim, the resulting explosion could produce an unpleasant shock.

When Margie was nearly six, Jack informed her that she would be having a party because you always did on your birthday. There had been no mention of this at home so Margie wasn't completely convinced, but he was so confident of the event that it seemed churlish not to invite him.

He arrived on the doorstep in time for tea, washed and brushed and wearing a clean jersey. But alas! there was no party. Mother was first astonished, then very cross (with Margie!) and finally embarrassed at what Mrs. Ambler would think when Jack returned home. In the end she felt constrained to give a birthday party, the only one Margie remembered having. It took place exactly a fortnight later on Dick's ninth birthday and was a joint affair, each of them being allowed to invite three friends.

Margie asked Mary, Gladys and Dorothy May from school so presumably Jack had to be one of Dick's guests. The birthday tea was served, not in the living kitchen, but in the back room. There was a bought cake, a unique treat in the Lumley household. It was large and rectangular with gold decorations on its chocolate-coated surface. Instead of crackers the girls were presented with fancy bonnets made of crepe paper and the boys with Red Indian braves' head-dresses, complete with feathers.

From that moment the uneasy liaison between the sexes came to an abrupt end and segregation was the order of the day. The boys swarmed to a vantage point on the garden wall overlooking the back street and, ignoring the bonneted maidens demurely awaiting them in the yard, proceeded to intimidate all comers with blood-curdling war cries.

Jack didn't go to St. Luke's Sunday School as Dick and Margie did, but attended the Wesleyans', which must be superior, Margie thought, because membership entitled you to a star card. Jack took his with him every Sunday and had an asterisk stamped on it to signify attendance. As if such glory were not enough, it transpired that the Sunday School secretary who stamped the cards was no less a person than Mr. Clegg, the Geography master at Belle Vue.

Nothing but a star card would now satisfy Margie but this coveted status symbol could be obtained only by attendance at the Wesleyan Sunday School. After a prolonged tussle Mother finally gave in and let her go. Bursting with pride she marched into the secretary's office to witness the stamping of the first precious star inside the folded blue card.

At the Wesleyans' every class had the luxury of a separate room opening off the assembly hall. Here they retired with their teacher when the preliminaries were over. The Wesleyans also had Guides and Brownies. Margie was a romantic child who loved fairy tales and had always wanted to be an ethereal creature with delicate gossamer wings. When she found out that some Brownies were fairies, a star card was no longer sufficient: she must join the Brownies and become a fairy.

Unfortunately there was no room in the Fairy Six so she had to be an elf with a grotesque green figure dancing on the pocket of her uniform. Brown Owl, earnest and freckled with sandy hair and glasses, wearing a navy uniform and a felt hat turned up at one side, taught her the Brownie Law and Promise and showed her how to make a plait, and she was enrolled. Dancing round the toadstool was all right but unfortunately the main activity of the evening for each Six seemed to be the sandpapering of a box, which wasn't Margie's idea of fun.

Even so, there were compensations. The Brownies were to perform at a garden party held on the daisy-starred lawns of a large house where one of the church bigwigs lived. Dancing in a green elfin costume with Phrygian cap and bells was one thing, but getting in and out of it behind the shrubbery on a sweltering day, even with help from Mother and Auntie, was quite another. The tight cotton leotard with attached hood had to be pulled on, feet first, over one's socks and shoes and, in Margie's case at least, far too much protective underwear, and was uncomfortably claustrophobic.

The elfin dance was repeated at the Christmas Fair held in the schoolroom. In addition to the twin attractions of Father Christmas **and** a bran tub, there was country dancing by the Guides, the "men" wearing rustic smocks and breeches and floppy hats and the "women" in flowered frocks and sunbonnets. It was Margie's introduction to folk dancing and she was entranced by the gay music and patterns of rings and lines and squares that evolved as the dancers skipped and linked arms and wove a hey.

Brown Owl had promised to take the Brownies one Saturday afternoon on an outing to Shipley Glen. Margie's recollections of a previous blissful visit were not of moorland, rock and stream but of the popular **Glen Tramway**, the **Cape to Cairo Railway** and the swings and roundabouts in the Japanese Gardens. So she put on her best coat and Sunday hat trimmed with rosettes of brown ribbon. Probably because of the unsettled weather, only three Brownies presented themselves at the appointed meeting place. The other two were more suitably clad in their Brownie dresses and Brown Owl was wearing her navy uniform.

After a tram ride and a considerable walk, they reached the top of the glen just as torrential rain began to fall. Perhaps it was out of consideration for Margie's best hat that Brown Owl took them into a farmhouse where shyly they drank tea and nibbled cakes.

By the time the rain had abated, it was too late to go farther up the glen. Instead they actually went on the rocking boat and swings in the Japanese Gardens and paddled a flat-bottomed craft on the tiny ornamental lake. Best of all, they each had a turn on the **Cape to Cairo Railway.** Chained into large chairs fixed to an overhead cable, they swung dizzily, one after another, down the slope and round a hairpin bend and were deposited, a few breathless seconds later, at the terminus far below their starting point.

It was not until Brown Owl was saying goodbye to her charges outside the Wesleyan chapel that Margie remembered her hat. She had last seen it hanging by its elastic from the back of a seat before she went on the **Cape to Cairo Railway.** It speaks volumes for Brown Owl's devotion to duty that, having first taken Margie home and explained the situation, she went straight back to the glen, returning in weary triumph with the hat long after Margie had gone to bed.

Shrove Tuesday brought fresh vigour to the life of the street, muted during the rain and slush of the winter months. Hens were laying, the sap was beginning to rise and, moved by some atavistic instinct, every boy brought out his whip and top, though back yards afforded a better space for spinning than the uneven setts of the street.

The large iron hoop bowled along with the aid of a stick was already obsolete and hoots of derision greeted Bert Harrop's brief appearance with one. But marbles were always in fashion. Common-or-garden opaque coloured taws weren't highly prized but the real beauties, the expensive translucent glass alleys streaked with spiralling multi-coloured threads, were much coveted.

Piggy was a popular game with the boys. The equipment needed was a long stick and a much shorter, thicker bit of wood, four or five inches long, whittled smooth with a point at either end till it resembled a torpedo. This was the piggy. Most boys made their own from a chip of firewood.

The piggy was placed on the ground and rapped smartly at one end with the longer stick till it flew in the air. It was then given a mighty swipe with the long stick. The competitor whose piggy travelled the farthest distance was the winner.

Whips and tops and marbles and piggy were mainly for boys. The girls became adept at ball games ranging from the simple to the complicated. Traditional nonsense rhymes accompanied many of the games.

Skipping could be an individual or a communal activity. Margie's special skipping rope had red, white and blue striped handles with bells which rang as she skipped. The most common skipping exercise was "Pitch, patch, pepper", two slow skips being followed by as many fast skips or **peppers** as you could manage before your feet tangled with the rope. Even more skill and considerably more practice were required for skipping backwards or with hands crossed.

The favourite skipping game, played exclusively by girls, was a kind of fortune telling. You skipped slowly through the questions and peppered very fast through the answers till you were out at some fateful letter, number or word. The exciting part was choosing the name of your intended husband to the accompaniment of a good deal of giggling from your friends. Margie loved this thrilling game of make-believe and took it very seriously.

> "Raspberry, strawberry, gooseberry jam,
> Tell me the name of your young man!
> > A, B, C, D ...
> "What is his surname?
> > A, B, C, D ...
> "When will you marry?
> > January, February ...
> "What will the bride wear?
> > Silk, satin, muslin, rags,
> > Silk, satin ...
> "What will she ride in?
> > Coach, carriage, wheelbarrow, muck-cart,
> > Coach, carriage ...

"How many bridesmaids?
    One, two, three ...
"What will you live in?
    Palace, mansion, cottage, hovel,
    Palace, mansion ...
"How many children?
    One, two, three ..." and so on.

Occasionally the "tarts", as the boys inexplicably called the girls, were allowed to join in the boys' games. They could even play at **Cowboys and Indians** provided, that is, they agreed to be Indians. The boys must be cowboys because, of course, they always won.

The start of every game was interminably delayed by the momentous business of deciding who should be "it". This was done by a process called **dipping**. The players stood in a ring, one of them pointing to each of the others in turn as she recited, perhaps,

    "Dash! dash! dash!
    My blue sash
    Sailing on the water!
    Dash, dash! dash!
    And **you** shall **not** be 'it'!"

Boys, of course, would never use "Dash! dash! dash!" The favourite eliminating rhyme was undoubtedly "One potato". Each child in the group held out his clenched fists and the administrator of the rhyme went round the circle, thumping each fist, including his own, as he recited:

    "**One** potato, **two** potato, **three** potato, **four,**
    Five potato, **six** potato, **seven** potato **more.**"

The fist he struck on the word "more" went behind the owner's back and, when both your fists had been struck out, you were eliminated. The owner of the last fist left was "it".

The two most popular back street games were **Relievo!** and **Tin Can Squat.** Both meant trespassing in other back yards as there was nowhere else to hide. Margie would tingle with fear as, in the reassuring company of Lizzie Harrop or Jack Ambler, she crept into the dusty garden belonging to Mr. Trewavas, the irascible retired solicitor, or braved the wrath of the two elderly maiden ladies who had an unpleasant habit of spying through the heavy wooden slats of their Venetian blinds before darting out of the back door to pounce on an unwary intruder.

The object of **Relievo!** was to rescue any of your chums who had been discovered and were languishing in the enemy den, before he who was "it" caught **you. Tin Can Squat,** the most popular game of all, was a variation on this theme. The obvious pre-requisite was an old tin can. Some Hercules would kick it as far as possible, thus giving all the players the chance to run off and hide ... all, that is, save the unfortunate child who was "it". **He** had to retrieve the can and replace it in the middle of the street before turning to his main task of rounding up the concealed players. The daredevil who managed to slip unseen from his hiding place to administer another mighty kick to the can gave a new lease of life to those of his comrades who had already been discovered. In fact, everybody could look for a new hidey-hole while poor "it" was chasing after the can and restoring it to its rightful place.

Part of the inherited mystique of back street games was the magic word "barley" or "barlo!" Uttering this word (while hopping on one leg with two fingers crossed) was a request for respite on the part of the pursued that could not be ignored. After a brief uncomfortable truce the struggle would be resumed.

Chapter Thirteen

Visitors

Grannie and Grandad had three married sons still living in Bradford who paid sporadic visits to the household in Leamington Street. Uncle Arthur and his wife and her sister would drop in from time to time and certainly never missed Christmas Day. Mother would remark tartly to Grannie that no doubt Arthur had come for something to eat.

He was her second eldest brother, a tall, goodlooking man, bluff and hearty with twinkling blue eyes. In his late thirties, at a double wedding with Mother and Dad, he had married Alice Crabtree, a pretty young woman with a carefully cultivated air of gentility.

Uncle Arthur had trained as a cabinet maker but, like so many in the trade, found himself on short time in the twenties. He and his wife and her sister existed rather than lived in a cold, gloomy back-to-back house in downtown Clarendon Street, where there was scarcely a flicker of fire in the grate or a crumb of food on the table.

For besides being prim and pretty, Aunt Alice was also stingy and a saver. Before she would consent to marry him, Uncle Arthur had had to promise to neither drink nor smoke in future. As they had no children, perhaps the ban had extended even farther. Mother felt sorry for her genial brother and thought he'd been a fool to fall for a pretty face.

At Christmas when the sherry and port wine were brought round, Aunt Alice, bridling delicately, would say to her husband in a tight little voice, "Remember your promise, Arthur!"

She and her sister paid not the slightest heed to fashion. New clothes and the latest hair styles cost money, and money was something to be hoarded, not spent. At a time when most women of their age were bobbed or shingled, they still wore their long hair looped up in Edwardian fashion. No matter that the hemline had shot up to the knees as the waistline dropped to the hips: they still came to visit wearing high-necked blouses under antediluvian dark serge costumes with wasp-waisted, hip-length jackets and full skirts that swept the floor. Mother and Auntie were hardly slavish followers of exaggerated contemporary styles but at least they didn't look figures of fun as the aunts undoubtedly did.

The unmarried sister, "Aunt" Emma, was a pleasant, modest and intelligent woman whom Mother held in high esteem. She had left the mill for a job on the Home and Colonial stall in the Rawson Market in town. But her sensitive soul shrank from carrying out her instructions to advertise the wares by bawling at the potential customer like any street pedlar.

Uncle Walter was another occasional visitor. Shrunken, insignificant and almost toothless, he was unrecognisable as the handsome young man who had posed with his good-looking bride for their wedding photograph twenty years earlier. He had been apprenticed to a brass-founder but an accident at work, in which a fragment of metal lodged in his eye, had seriously affected his sight and now he seemed to be "allus lakin", as he put it.

Aunt Adelaide and he had had a number of children of whom only three survived. Hilda had married and emigrated to Australia. The other two much younger children were boys about the same age as Dick and Margie. They were usually brought to show their new Whit Sunday suits to Grannie and Grandad and never went home without a penny or even a silver "threepenny dodger" in the pocket.

Their parents had never recovered from the financial problems caused by their early marriage and Uncle Walter's accident, and Aunt Adelaide had to work in the mill for most of her married life. They lived in a downtown slum called White Abbey. The family was never formally invited there but Mother sometimes made a detour on her way home from town to call and see how they were, often taking Margie with her.

Margie hated it. Two steep steps sticking right out on the causeway led to the front door. This gave directly on to the one living room. Its most prominent piece of furniture was a large bed with brass knobs in which lay Aunt Adelaide's mother, a shrunken woman of ninety with snow-white hair and a flaking complexion of a startling pink.

Mother and Dad had the most rapport with Uncle Bill and Aunt Ada whose only child, Cousin Willie, was the same age as Margie. Uncle Bill bore no resemblance to the dapper young man who had posed self-consciously in his new suit for the family photograph in 1910. He had been gassed while serving with the army in Flanders and suffered for the rest of his life from stomach trouble. Sallow, haggard and always ailing, he seemed much older than Mother though he was actually a year or so younger.

The children sometimes overheard him talking about the war, which Dad hardly ever did. He would light cigarettes for Dad and Georgie, then deliberately blow out the match and strike another for his own cigarette, remarking gloomily, "Third man dies!"

Uncle Bill said you got very superstitious in the trenches. In his sector, mule trains were used to convey supplies to the front line. The mules could be very stubborn and it was quite a job to urge them on round one notorious corner through the flying shrapnel and whistling bullets. Once a chap lost his nerve, said Uncle Bill, he was done for.

"Take this snapshot (or letter or wedding ring)," a soldier due to go with the mule train would say to his pal, "and if anything happens to me, see that it gets to my wife."

It was no good trying to cheer up a chap who felt like that, said Uncle Bill, or to dissuade him from parting with his keepsakes. He never came back.

"They had a premonition, you see," he concluded in lugubrious tones.

He told other macabre stories unconnected with the war. Most of them concerned the French polishing of coffins which was often done with the body already inside. One time, he joked, the corpse sat up and he had a job to push it down again. But it was no joke that a skilled cabinet maker and French polisher, whose health had been undermined by trench warfare so that he was unable to hold down a full-time job, should receive not one penny in compensation or pension.

Cousin Willie was a stolid, red-cheeked boy, excessively coddled by his mother because she said he suffered from bronchitis. There was always a great bulge under his jacket where a knitted scarf was folded across his bad chest.

Aunt Ada thought him very clever and, at the slightest sign of encouragement, would get him to recite his party piece, Kipling's "Big Steamers". Margie had heard it so often, she could almost join in. She felt somehow inferior to think that at Drummond Road they had never come across what must obviously be a masterpiece.

Clearing his throat and assuming his special elocution voice, Cousin Willie would open his mouth wide and begin, in a mood of high solemnity, his stilted dialogue with the monarchs of the ocean.

> "'O where are you going to, all you big steamers,
> With England's own coal, up and down the salt seas?'
> 'We are going to fetch you your bread and your butter,
> Your beef, pork and bacon, eggs, apples and cheese.'"

And so at last to the conclusion which never failed to send a shiver of foreboding down Margie's spine. Cousin Willie's voice deepened dramatically as he uttered the grave exhortation:

"'Send out your big warships to guard your great waters
That no-one may stop us from bringing you food.

"'For the bread that you eat and the biscuits you nibble,
The sweets that you suck and the joints that you carve,
Are brought to you daily by all us Big Steamers ...
And if anyone hinders our coming, YOU'LL STARVE!'"

And a complacent Cousin Willie would sit down, modestly unmoved by the dire warning he had just delivered.

Margie was fond of her cousin and liked going to Uncle Bill's though it was a long walk to the terrace of tall, gaunt houses in Girlington.

The ramshackle greenhouse built on at the back was a great attraction. From a horticultural point of view it was a desert for Uncle Bill was seldom well enough to bother with it, but Margie and Cousin Willie used it as their house when they played at being married. Under the benevolently indulgent eye of the adults, he would kiss her goodbye and go off on his motor-bike (the garden seat), emitting an appropriate assortment of growling and screeching noises, while Margie stayed more or less contentedly at home in the greenhouse, dusting the wilting pot plants and thinking not at all of her infidelity to her other husband, Jack Ambler.

Chapter Fourteen

Friends ... and Foes!

The first class in the "big school" was taught by Miss Craven, a plump, elderly woman with broken veins in her cheeks and faded auburn hair pinned back in a bun.

Margie wrote her first composition in Miss Craven's class. It consisted of three sentences on the absorbing subject, "My best hat" (the one retrieved from Shipley Glen by Brown Owl). Not for Miss Craven the uninhibited, unpunctuated outpourings of the present day! No matter how jerky the style or how banal the subject matter, the composition was entirely satisfactory as long as the spelling, grammar and punctuation were faultless and the writing copperplate.

Everybody knitted in Miss Craven's class: half a pink woolly vest! Perhaps a complete vest per child had been intended but no pattern shows up mistakes so clearly as a "knit two, seam two" rib, and doubtless Miss Craven grew tired of pulling back and putting right the work at night like some latter-day Penelope. When the pieces (ranging in shade from dusty pink to mid-charcoal) were at last finished, she stitched them together in twos (back and front identical) and parents were invited to purchase the resulting tubular products.

With only half as many vests on sale as children in the class, it was fortunate that there was no great rush to buy. Much to Margie's disappointment Mother, an accomplished and meticulous knitter, recoiled in horror from the idea of buying a vest, only **half** of which, at the most, **might** have been knitted by her daughter, and the other half possibly by some dirty, itching ragamuffin from White Abbey.

The girls had their first ever sewing lesson with Miss Craven. Each child was solemnly warned to be very careful with her needle, to fasten it into her work when she had finished, and on no account to lose it. The warning was reinforced by a graphic account of how a foolish girl had actually swallowed one and been made to eat cotton-wool sandwiches to prevent it perforating her vital parts in transit.

At first all went well apart from some inevitable spotting of the work with blood from pricked fingers. Then Kinking Freda couldn't find her needle. Miss Craven having already implanted the idea in her mind, she announced automatically that she had swallowed it. A thorough search revealed no needle: pandemonium ensued and the head teacher was summoned. Freda, a spindly child with wisps of flaxen hair, obliged with an unsolicited demonstration of her breath-taking (or rather breath-holding) powers before being whisked off to the children's hospital.

For the rest of the afternoon a subdued Standard One huddled over its desks in a state of shocked paralysis, contemplating the unimaginable horrors of X-rays, operating theatres and cotton-wool sandwiches. In a moment of anti-climax during clearing-up operations at the close of the afternoon, the missing needle came to light. It had been lying on Freda's desk under her sewing all the time!

Drummond Road was regarded, at least by its own staff and pupils and their parents, as the best elementary school in the city. It invariably achieved excellent results in the all-important annual scholarship exam.

The head teacher, Miss Parkin, had been awarded the M.B.E. for her services to education. With her crooked mouth and twisted face (the aftermath of a stroke) surmounted by a quantity of frizzy hair, dyed red and encircled by a black velvet band, she would have presented a formidable enough appearance to her scholars without the thick stick she always carried and used to such effect. Even well-behaved children felt its stinging impact more than once in the course of their few years under her tutelage. As she also regularly sported a blazer of a loud vermilion that clashed with the auburn of her hennaed hair, her aspect was not only frightening but positively bizarre.

Margie made new friends in the big school. But the friendship which for a brief period had the greatest impact on her life was that with Lizzie Harrop from down the street. As Lizzie was Margie's senior by more than twelve months, she was very flattered at being thus singled out.

Lizzie was in the class taught by Miss Bell, one of the legion of spinsters responsible for education in the twenties. She was a long thin woman who affected purple dresses and wore round her long thin neck a tight black velvet ribbon with attached cameo brooch.

Not only did the two girls walk to and from school together: Lizzie also invited Margie to call for her in a morning. So as soon as the mill buzzer had blared half-past eight, Margie would set off for the Harrops' house a few doors further down the street.

Lizzie was never ready so Margie had to stand about awkwardly in the kitchen while the family finished breakfast in her presence. At home this was a scrappy meal as members of the household left for work at different times. But in the Harrop ménage the whole family sat down at the table together.

And while the main dish at home was bread and dripping, with Dick and Margie wrangling over their share of the tasty brown jelly from the bottom of the stone jar, the Harrops ate what was to Margie an untried delicacy, porridge.

She would watch in fascinated wonder as the pallid mixture was ladled out by Mrs. Harrop, a thin, exhausted woman with her hair permanently tied in curl rags. It was handed round the table by Auntie, her spinster sister who fulfilled in the family the role of household drudge.

Mr. Harrop, a Dickensian figure, presided at the head of the table, monitoring the behaviour of his brood. He was a stout, red-faced but far from jovial man who sported a bowler hat, not just on Sunday mornings when herding his flock to church, but also during the week when bound for the office.

Bert, the eldest child, was sufficiently intelligent to keep on the right side of his father as well as the staff at school, and astute enough, when involved in trouble, to make sure that, no matter who took the blame, **he** was never found out.

Besides Lizzie herself and Stan, a pleasant, friendly lad the same age as Margie, there were the pre-school-age twins, Flossie and Joey, the one as plump as the other was scrany. Joey was a strange, dark, pasty-faced, lisping child who had difficulty in making himself understood. He had a reputation for wandering off and getting lost. On one occasion when the police joined his father in an all-night search for him, the hue and cry made headlines in the local paper. He was discovered fast asleep in the cab of a lorry in which he had earlier been given a joy-ride.

Because of her enforced weekly attendances at church Lizzie could rattle off from memory large chunks of the order of service for Morning Prayer and even a few portentous responses from the Litany. Margie, who went only occasionally with Dad to the Congs. on Sunday evenings and even less often with Auntie to St. Luke's, was astounded at the extent of Lizzie's knowledge and in comparison felt a complete ignoramus.

The whole Harrop family seemed to have its ear to the ground and

84

never missed any local event. Lizzie came round one evening to persuade Margie to go with her to a concert at the Congregational chapel down Oak Lane.

"It's free! We can go in for nothing," she wheedled.

Against her better judgment Mother yielded to Margie's entreaties and allowed her to go.

It certainly was a ripping concert. They sat right at the front of the schoolroom among a crowd of children. Somebody sang "My bonny lies over the ocean" (**my bonny what**? chafed a critical Margie) and someone else made the astounding assertion that, sooner than sleep in a feather bed in a castle, she would lie down in a cold, open field along with the raggle-taggle gypsies.

The highlight of the concert was the most hackneyed of all pantomime routines. Two comedians sitting on a bench were approached from the rear by a third figure dressed as the devil in a lurid green mask with horns. Although the comedians seemed unaware of his presence, the audience were acutely conscious of it. Having first scared off one of his victims, the devil took his place beside the second who was supposedly ignorant of what had transpired.

The excited children at the front of the audience grew almost hysterical in their attempts to warn the stupid fellow of the danger he was in, but all in vain. Of course, he at length realised who his companion was and made a wild dash off stage, hotly pursued by Old Nick.

As the concert came to an end, the children became aware of a man coming round with a plate. You could go in for nothing, as Lizzie had said, but she hadn't mentioned the collection.

Margie hadn't a farthing on her. She felt guilty and frightened as the steward approached; the look of disgust that came over his face when she shook her head at the proffered plate heightened her sense of shame and humiliation. It was Lizzie who had got her into this embarrassing predicament. She could feel the tears pricking behind her eyes.

The Harrop children had no money, either, but they reacted to the situation with their usual brash nonchalance. Margie couldn't help feeling that they had gone there, knowing all along that there would be a collection.

There was Mother to face when she got home. Predictably, she was disgusted at her daughter going to an entertainment without paying, though she had to admit that it was hardly Margie's fault.

85

"Those Harrops! Always on the look-out for something for nothing!" was her verdict on the affair.

One very hot afternoon as a few children were playing out in listless fashion, one of the boys came tearing down the back street. When he had got his breath back, he poured out the startling news that a man had collapsed just down the road because of the heat wave, and that he was dead.

All the boys rushed off so as not to miss the sight.

"Come on!" said Lizzie. "Let's go as well!"

Margie hesitated. If she asked Mother's permission, she knew very well what she would say.

"You stay here and mind your own business!"

Stifling her conscience, Margie ran down the street after her friend. They could see the crowd the minute they turned the corner into Oak Lane. Apart from one or two irresponsible small boys darting excitedly hither and thither, they stood quiet and respectful in the presence of death, politely awaiting events.

On the far causeway in front of the Congregational chapel a couple of policemen in uniform were mounting guard over something that was lying on the ground, covered by a light brown coat.

The ambulance drew up as Lizzie and Margie came panting on the scene. The overcoat was removed and they caught a brief glimpse of a white-faced man with thinning grey hair. He was lying quite still as though in a different world from the self-important constables, the bustling ambulance men and the murmuring crowd.

The doors banged, the ambulance drove off and the spectators began to drift away. Limp and subdued, Margie and Lizzie started up the hill in the sweltering heat and trailed slowly and thoughtfully back home.

All at once the walks to and from school became fraught with danger. It was something to do with a gang of girls who had sworn to "get" Lizzie … and Margie as well, her new-found crony informed her with some urgency, simply because she was Lizzie's friend.

Instead of going home the usual way along Conduit Street and through the two snickets into Oak Lane, they had to use devious routes to avoid any encounter with the gang. Margie didn't know any of the girls personally but the mere thought of them terrified her, while the hiding round corners and dodging down alleyways turned every journey home into a nightmare.

86

One afternoon they had decided to nonplus their enemies by going home the long way round via Silver Street and Heaton Road. They were hurrying down Oak Lane, no more than a stone's throw from Leamington Street, when Lizzie caught sight of one of the gang. Immediately they left the main road and raced along a side street. Now only one snicket lay between them and home. As they turned the corner with safety so near, out stepped the gang and barred their way.

They tried to turn back but others who had been following closed in from the rear. They were trapped. The six or eight girls hemmed them in until they were huddled ignominiously together with their backs to the wall.

It was an experience Margie never forgot. Accusations from the gang flew about, interspersed with vigorous denials and counter-accusations from Lizzie. The air was thick with threats of hair-pulling and other less specified acts of violence.

Eventually the gang fell to arguing among themselves about the fate of their victims. Spying a gap in their squabbling ranks, Lizzie, ever an opportunist, shouted, "Run for it!"

Margie needed no second bidding. With a desperation born of sheer panic she broke through the opposing array and tore down the snicket and along Leamington Street to her own front gate. There was no sign of Lizzie or anyone else behind her but she dared not embark on the considerable detour required to reach home the usual way along the back street. She leapt up the steps and pulled on the bell.

The front door was hardly ever used as it opened on to the floor above the back kitchen where the family spent most of its time. You might go out the front way at the weekend en route for the park or a service at St. Luke's, but the back door served for everyday use.

For what seemed an eternity Margie stood gasping on the front steps. Her heart was thudding fit to burst and her throat felt like sandpaper. Every few moments she cast an anxious glance behind. Surely they wouldn't attack her on her own doorstep!

No-one came. Perhaps the bell didn't work. In desperation she pulled it again. She knew her legs wouldn't carry her all the way round by the back street.

At last she heard the sound of approaching footsteps. The chain was taken off, the heavy bolt drawn back, and the key grated in the lock. There stood Mother, out of breath after toiling up a flight of stairs and along the passage, and looking none too pleased when she saw who had summoned her.

Her indignant grumbles were followed, the minute Margie got down to the kitchen, by a few acid comments from Grannie. In the inquest which inevitably ensued, the whole story came out and a tearful Margie was forbidden to go to and from school with Lizzie Harrop again.

Somehow she never did. The omniscient Lizzie, revealed as a silly, squabbling girl who had most likely brought her troubles on herself, had fallen from her pedestal. The brief alliance was at an end.

Chapter Fifteen

Goddesses

A wave of excitement surged through Standard 2A at the start of their second year in the big school. They were to have a new teacher fresh from college.

Miss Broadbent couldn't have been more than twenty. She was tall and pretty and wore her straight brown hair fashionably bobbed with a fringe. Right from the start 2A were her infatuated worshippers. She was not only much younger and far more attractive than any other teacher in the school: she was also much less strict a disciplinarian.

Silence wasn't strictly enforced in Miss Broadbent's classroom on sewing afternoons. She allowed a little quiet conversation and even chatted to the girls herself. Some of the bolder spirits cajoled her into telling them what life was like at the all-female teacher training college she had so recently left.

It was injudicious of her to relate anecdotes, no matter how innocuous, to an audience of eight-year-olds. On one occasion, for example, she was in her friend's room during prohibited hours when footsteps were heard approaching and there was a knock on the door. She had barely time to dive into the wardrobe before the college principal, who was paying a round of calls on her students, made a stately entrance. The concealed miscreant was not only able to remain undetected in the wardrobe throughout the principal's visit: she even managed to steal down the corridor and back to her room in time for her own visitation. The class was agog with excitement during the narration and astonished at its idol's daring.

It was a momentous day when Miss Broadbent invited eight of her class to stay behind for half an hour after school. Intrigued and excited, they spent the afternoon making wild guesses at what might be required of them. When the other children had been dismissed, she took them into the main hall.

"How would you like to learn folk dancing?" she asked, moving gracefully from one foot to the other as she spoke, then twirling nimbly round.

How **would** they! The chosen eight, flattered already at being singled out for the goddess's special favour, were at once thrown into a fever of excitement. Margie glowed with sheer happiness as she remembered the Guides' dancing at St. John's Christmas Fair.

Lessons started straight away and the eight soon learned how to side and arm, set and turn single, dance a hey, lead up a double and fall back a double. Mother bought Margie some bronze dancing slippers with a long piece of fine elastic to twist in a figure of eight over her white socks. For a time at least, they displaced even Sunshine Susie's high heels in her affections.

As first couple Millicent and Margie had the distinction of leading the team of dancers in **The Black Nag** and **Goddesses.** Millicent, a willowy wraith with a cloud of dark hair, took the part of first man as she was the taller, and Margie danced first woman.

Millicent's friend, Mabel, a tall, graceful girl with a sweet disposition, was another member of the group. She and Millicent were only children; like others in the class, they had lost their fathers in the war, and each lived with her mother and grannie. Mabel was partnered by Katie, a robust tomboy with straight sandy hair and freckles.

Two of the dances they learned were the set pieces for a competition held annually in Roundhay Park, Leeds, on what was known as Children's Day. Much to their excitement, it was decided that the group should represent the school at this event.

The great day dawned warm and sunny. A number of relatives and friends including Mother and Auntie and Baby, who was four, were among the party. Margie had never been to Leeds though it was only nine miles off.

The competition was held on the flat octagonal roof of the boathouse, a site so tiny that it was almost impossible for anyone but the judges to get near enough to see the display. But Miss Broadbent was delighted when her team of raw recruits, competing in public for the first time, was awarded third prize.

In the autumn the same group took part in a festival at the Huddersfield Town Hall. On this occasion they blossomed forth in identical pale mauve frocks trimmed with white, made by proud mothers, aunts and grannies. Fidgeting uneasily, the young Bradfordians huddled together watching the other competitors from a vantage point on the tiers of seats below the towering pipe organ.

The two set dances, **The Health** and **Maid in the Moon,** each for four couples, were much more difficult than the beginners' dances they had learned earlier in the year. Their spirits dropped as they realised how high was the standard being set by other competitors.

But worse was to come. By some misunderstanding Miss Broadbent hadn't brought a pianist with her, assuming that one would be provided. This was not the case. Eventually a scratch pianist volunteered his services but it was obvious the moment he started to play that the girls wouldn't stand a chance. They had to dance virtually in slow motion to keep in time with his dragging tempo and, though the judges commiserated with them, this time there was no prize.

Folk dancing wasn't the only innovation launched by Miss Broadbent. At Christmas, with the help of Standard 2A, she presented a pageant of the seasons before the assembled school. There was no stage in the main hall but that hardly mattered as little dramatic skill was required for what was no more than a series of recitations.

Twelve girls had been chosen to represent the months of the year. As far as possible each had been allocated her birthday month and was to deliver a monologue of rhyming couplets in its praise. So it was Millicent, bewitching in party frock and spangles as icy January, on whom fell the glory of opening the proceedings.

There were so many performers with September birthdays that some of them had perforce to represent other months. An unwilling and disappointed Margie had to accept the role of August, **faute de mieux**. Wearing nothing more dashing than cotton frocks, she and Mabel, who was born in July, appeared together in a dialogue that ran something like this:

Margie: August is my name and I ...
Mabel: I speak first; I am July.
Both: Hand in hand we come. Because ...
Margie: We together on our ways
Scatter summer holidays.
Mabel: All the joys that we unfold
Children would not change for gold.
Margie: Nor would teachers, I am told.
Mabel: Boating 'mid the lily pads,
Swimming, fishing, for the lads ...

And so on. The pageant reached a climax with the entrance of a heavily disguised figure wearing a cotton-wool beard, enveloped in a hooded scarlet cloak trimmed with more cotton-wool, and carrying a cardboard sickle. It was Miss Broadbent herself in the role of Father Time.

In spite of stage fright, the performers were thrilled by the occasion. It was, as far as they could remember, the one and only end-of-term entertainment ever presented during the four years they spent in the big school.

Family Group 1910

(left to right, back row)
Uncle Joe   Aunt Jinny (Uncle Harry's Wife)   Uncle George   Aunt Ada   Uncle Arthur
(middle row)
Mother (Nellie)   Grandfather   Grandmother   Uncle Bill   Aunt Emily
(front row)
                    Hilda (cousin aged 10)   Auntie Annie

Chapter Sixteen

Nemesis

It had been a carefree year for Miss Broadbent's class. But they were in for a rude awakening. At the end of the year Standard 2A was split up.

A lucky few who included Millicent and Mabel were despatched to 3A and kindly Miss Margerison. But a grimmer fate awaited the rest. They were going into 3B ... to set an example, the head teacher explained. For them Nemesis waited in the shape of Miss Preece, the school's strictest disciplinarian.

It was a disgrace to be in a 'B' class, no matter what Miss Parkin said. Miss Broadbent's quondam goddesses sat shivering like mere mortals in the new classroom. Above them hung the familiar opaque globes of the gaslights. To their left the inevitable row of aspidistras flourished on the windowsill. But straight ahead loomed the terrifying though fascinating figure of Miss Preece, the unknown quantity.

Small, stocky and bow-legged, the figure was unprepossessing enough. Miss Preece wore a mud-coloured skirt and matching cardigan. She was dark, sallow and undeniably plain. Though the class thought her elderly, she was probably no more than forty.

Her gimlet eyes probed to the core of each individual cowering before her. At once the hope and despair of the school, they had been lumped together to be kneaded and pounded into that desirable substance, scholarship material. And who more suited to the task than the formidable Miss Preece?

Her approach to discipline was simple. She would pounce on a likely victim and reduce her to tears with a few well-chosen words of ridicule. This virtually ensured the rest of the class trying by every means to avoid similar humiliation.

There was also, of course, the cane!

Freda the Kinker had come into 3B, bringing with her her reputation. Oh, yes! Miss Preece had heard of Freda! As the Kinker's eyes filled with ready tears, the class stirred, anticipating yet another of the masterly exhibitions of convulsive sobbing, gasping for breath, and eventual turning blue in the face which made up the dread stock-in-trade of the redoubtable Freda.

But she had no time to get under way.

"I give you a solemn warning," snarled the dragon, "that if you start kinking in this class, I shall drag you outside, sit you down on the concrete floor and throw cold water over you. That'll teach you to hold your breath!"

Not a child doubted that, if the need arose, she would be as good as her word ... least of all Freda. And though during the next two years she was caned regularly, she never kinked. Her face would crumple with suppressed agony and the tears brim her eyes as she clutched her smarting hand, but a stern reminder was enough to quell any exhibition of temper.

There were several new girls in the class: they had previously attended Midland Road School which took pupils only to the age of nine. One of them, a quiet, dark, handsome girl called Clare, was to be for years Margie's friend and rival. Another, Winnie, a tense, lively, white-faced child, was later much given to daring whispers and nudges when the dragon's back was turned. But for the moment they were new girls, strange and frightened.

Miss Preece disliked having intruders from what she considered an inferior school thrust into her class. She ordered Winnie and Clare to stand up, and made no bones about telling them how badly they had been taught. She would have her work cut out, she knew, to get them up to Drummond Road standards. But get them there she would, by hook or by crook. By the time the two were allowed to resume their seats, Clare was on the verge of tears and even dare-devil Winnie was twisting her hands in nervous apprehension.

Miss Preece was soon proved wrong. The two had been given a solid grounding and Clare, in particular, proved an outstanding pupil. But Miss Preece never forgave her the crime of being a Midland Road girl and criticised her work on every possible occasion.

Life in 3B was tough. Miss Preece was strict, thorough and absolutely single-minded in her determination to educate her charges. But even she had her Achilles heel. The class soon discovered that, like so many in her profession, she was in love with the sound of her own voice. Once get her astride a hobby-horse and they could sit back and relax till she was brought to earth by the ringing of the bell!

Prominent among her pet topics were health, punctuality and thoroughness. If a thing was worth doing at all, it was worth doing well.

Absence from school was a heinous crime equalled in magnitude only by unpunctuality. The cane was usually administered to late arrivals; even valid excuses were only grudgingly accepted. Woe betide the latecomer who had "been to the clinic with my leg, miss" or "with my eye, miss"!

"You wouldn't get far without it," Miss Preece would snort, effectively exposing the victim to the sniggers of her traitor peers.

It was customary for a class to be allowed home half an hour early on a Friday afternoon in the unlikely event of its having achieved 100% attendance throughout the week. This paltry carrot was so consistently dangled in front of the donkeys of 3B that absentees came to be regarded almost as delinquents.

It only confirmed their tendency to exaggerate the severity of the ailment that had kept them away. Unfortunate indeed the girl who had stayed at home with a bilious attack which she magnified into gastritis! Like many another perfectionist, the dyspeptic Miss Preece was a martyr to the complaint herself and would dismiss the sufferer's petty symptoms with contempt. The name she coined for all but terminal illnesses was "Don't-want-to-go-to-school-itis".

The day started with prayers in the main hall, taken by Miss Parkin. There were no hymnbooks. The words of the limited repertoire of hymns were gradually assimilated, not without error, over the four-year period. Was it, for example,

"Before the hills in order stood
Or earth received her **frame,**"

rather than

"Before the hills in order stood
Or earth received her **frade**"?

Which of these strange commodities, a **frame** or a **frade,** was earth more likely to have received? Even more puzzling was another hymn with the incomprehensible opening line,

"There is a book, who runs may read".

It was 1925 and disillusioned ex-servicemen were tramping the streets, hawking trifles from door to door. But patriotism had not yet become a dirty word. Kipling's **Recessional** was sung much at morning prayers if understood little. The "far-flung battle line" of "the captains and the kings" sounded magnificent and every child knew that Britain, with all those bits coloured pink on the map, was top nation.

The register taken, the next business was Scripture. Much attention

96

was paid to the Old Testament at the expense of the New: Miss Preece's favourite maxim wasn't "Love your enemies" but "An eye for an eye and a tooth for a tooth". Moses topped her popularity chart; this meant 3B memorising the ten plagues of Egypt in strict chronological order. Samuel, Saul, David and Jonathan were runners-up and, give or take a few passing references to Samson, Gideon and Elijah, the rest nowhere.

As for the New Testament, what with Disciples, Scribes and Pharisees, Publicans and Parables, none of them familiar concepts to a nine-year-old, it gave rise to even more confusion than did the nomadic Israelites' tortuous travels.

The books studied in English lessons were either abridged versions of, or selected passages from, the classics. Children figured prominently in all of them but a more miserable and down-trodden bunch of juveniles it would have been hard to find, from Pip and the Tulliver children (in **Great Expectations** and **The Mill on the Floss** respectively), beset by hordes of carping relatives and disagreeable acquaintances, to Tom, the wretched chimney sweep in **The Water Babies,** who escaped from Mr. Grimes only to fall into the clutches of Mrs. Be-done-by-as-you-did, a character with an uncomfortably close resemblance to Miss Preece herself.

Leigh Hunt's famous **Abou Ben Adhem** was a "must". So was Newbolt's no less celebrated **Vitaī Lampada,** though any link between the Close of privileged Clifton College in Bristol and 3B's classroom in Bradford's inner belt was limited to the "breathless hush" that at times pervaded both.

As the class had no poetry books, all extracts had to be written on the blackboard by their indefatigable teachers.

"O blithe newcomer!" they carolled with Wordsworth to a cuckoo whose song they had never heard.

"O to be in England!" they sighed with an Italian-based Browning though they had seen little more of it than the dark Satanic mills of their native city.

A purple passage from Scott's **Lay of the Last Minstrel,** which presumably encapsulated Miss Preece's patriotic sentiments, was dinned into 3B until they could recite it pat, though how much of it they really understood it would be hazardous to guess.

"Breathes there the man, with soul so dead,
Who never to himself hath said,
    This is my own, my native land!
Whose heart hath ne'er within him burn'd,
As home his footsteps he hath turn'd
    From wandering on a foreign strand!
If such there breathe, go mark him well;
For him no Minstrel raptures swell;
High though his titles, proud his name,
Boundless his wealth as wish can claim;
Despite those titles, power, and pelf,
The wretch, concentred all in self,
Living, shall forfeit fair renown,
And, doubly dying, shall go down
To the vile dust, from whence he sprung,
Unswept, unhonour'd and unsung."

Strong meat for nine-year-olds!

A Geography lesson with Miss Preece was nothing more than a series
of lists ... of mountains and rivers, capes and bays, counties, towns
and coalfields. The exact location of each had to be committed to
memory. This was difficult as there were neither text books nor
atlases. Equipment consisted of a large map of the British Isles which,
when hung up, almost covered the blackboard. It was too far off
and too shiny for the names on it to be decipherable. As Miss Preece
pointed out each place with the thick stick for which she often found
another use, her class of puppets had to identify it.

She invariably started with the capes and bays round the coastline
from Cape Wrath down to Beachy Head and back. Names of rivers
had to be memorised, especially those that flowed through Yorkshire
into the Humber estuary: Swale, Ure, Nidd, Wharfe, Aire, Ouse,
Calder, Don. Others of less importance (Thames, Mersey and Severn,
for example) were mentioned in passing.

Naturally Whernside, Ingleborough and Pen-y-ghent took pride of
place among the peaks. After them came less distinguished giants:
Ben Nevis; Helvellyn and Scafell; Snowden, Plynlimmon and Cader
Idris; Mam Tor and Brown Willy; and the final magnificent mouthful,
MacGillicuddy's Reeks in south-west Ireland.

Everybody in 3B knew where the Pennines were. Hadn't Miss Preece
told them over and over again that they ran down the middle of the
map, forming the backbone of England? But the class was utterly
confounded the day she asked them which way they would go, on
leaving the school premises, to find the Pennines?

This was mingling theory and practice with a vengeance. 3B were floored. A wild surmise leapt into Margie's head but was instantly suppressed: Miss Preece's mastery of the sarcastic rejoinder was such that one didn't volunteer an answer unless 100% certain it was right. She kept her own counsel.

"You're **on them!**" an exasperated Miss Preece exploded into the silence. "When you go home up Whetley Hill or down Carlisle Road, you'll be walking on the slopes of the Pennines. You **live** on them!"

3B struggled painfully with this staggering new thought. So they lived, not in a city full of smoking chimneys and smelly woollen mills, but on the backbone of England.

"And what," continued Miss Preece, determined to plumb the depths of their ignorance, "are the Pennines made of?"

Another poser! Grass and earth were half-heartedly suggested by some of the thicker-skinned.

"Millstone grit!" Miss Preece bellowed in triumph, almost as though she had herself created the chain of peaks. And so, she continued, were the people who lived on them. Strong, hardy, loyal and independent; not milksops or mollycoddles (two of her favourite words of opprobrium) like the folk who lived south of a line from Hull to Huddersfield. 3B eased themselves quietly into more comfortable positions and let the panegyric on their native county thunder over their heads. One could not imagine that, even in retirement, Miss Preece ever took part in the drift to the south.

In those days an elementary school teacher had to be a Jack-of-all-trades. The indomitable Miss Preece was no mere Jack but a master: singing, drawing, needlework and even games she took in her stride.

Equipment was minimal. For singing it consisted of a tuning fork and a modulator. Lessons were held in the classroom, the piano in the hall being used only at morning assembly. All words and music were laboriously chalked up on the blackboard, usually during playtime.

One never ceased to marvel at the tuning fork. Miss Preece had only to strike the top of her desk with its prongs and put them to her ear and, hey presto! she could conjure a note out of thin air.

Tonic sol-fa was the sole medium used. A long scroll (the modulator) was hung on the blackboard and, following the teachers's pointer as it hopped up and down, the class struggled to sing the notes she indicated from the range, **Doh ray mi fah soh lah te doh.** The exercise was made more difficult by the inclusion of semitones (**re, fe, se, ta** and so on) and there was sometimes a disastrous excursion into

99

the minor key (denoted by **lah te doh ray mi baa se lah**). To satisfy Miss Preece one had to open the mouth so wide as to be in danger of contracting lock-jaw; this no doubt helped in swallowing her acid comments on a flat and tuneless performance.

Some traditional songs had surprisingly lax moral standards. The young anti-hero of **Green Broom,** for example, was so lazy that, in order to get him out into the woods collecting broom, his aged father had to threaten to burn him in his bed. No sooner had the idle rascal started peddling the stuff through the streets than a wealthy lady of uncertain age, who had spied him from her window and been taken with his pleasing appearance, insisted that he come in, marry her forthwith and settle down to a life of luxury and ease. Such a reward for indolence was strangely out of keeping with Miss Preece's usual code of conduct and her many stern homilies on the value of industry, thrift and perseverance.

Other young gentlemen were impelled by even less worthy motives. In folk songs like **O where are you going to, my pretty little dear!** they deliberately set out to comb the countryside for rosy-cheeked milkmaids whom they might tempt from their bucolic employment with offers of silken gowns, coal-black steeds and gold and silver dainties. As the virtuous maidens preferred dabbling in the dew (whatever **that** might be) and invariably turned their backs on temptation, the innocents of 3B remained ignorant of the starker realities of life.

"Begone, dull care!" they carolled dutifully, "I prithee be gone from me!"

But singing with Miss Preece was never the joyful thing envisaged by William Byrd. Her carping attitude was so much at odds with the jovial words of the songs she was trying to teach that 3B found it impossible to "have a heart of harmless glee".

Besides all this, dangling over their heads like some ever-present sword of Damocles was the threat of Mr. Stork. What this bogeyman (the chief inspector of music for the Bradford schools) would think of their singing, Miss Preece dared not contemplate. He would be astonished and dismayed, appalled and horrified by the cacophony. A sense of foreboding settled on the class at the very mention of his name; they were unaware that inspectors came to inspect not so much the children as the teachers.

Mr. Stork never materialised but it was years before the bogey was laid. Around 1930 the city of Bradford presented a pageant in Peel Park to celebrate the jubilee of the granting of its charter. On the

100

day the Rt. Hon. David Lloyd George opened the proceedings, he was entertained by a large choir of children, among them several former members of Standard 3B at Drummond Road School, singing traditional songs. The jovial conductor who had trained the choir and with his entertaining personality had transformed singing to such a joyful thing was ... Mr. Stork!

Everybody had been ordered to bring a flower for the afternoon drawing lesson. But there were no flowers in the back yard nor even in the front garden, while a vase of flowers in the house was an unheard-of luxury. Margie grew so frantic at the thought of Miss Preece's wrath when she returned flowerless to school that Mother, grumbling mightily at the expense, was at last persuaded to thoil a copper or two to save her daughter from annihilation.

The Lumley household was thrown into an even greater flutter by another of Miss Preece's ideas. She told her class to take a good look at the lake in Manningham Park as they were to draw a picture of it from memory the following week. This simple instruction started a ferment. Every playtime was spent arguing about the shape of the lake, the position of its islands and the number of rowing boats that plied for hire.

The family tried in vain to convince Margie that what Miss Preece wanted was just a view of trees and water with a few swans and ducks swimming about. No-one was doing it like that, Margie stated firmly. She marched Auntie, Georgie and even Dad round the lake in turn to obtain their opinion of its irregular shape and the siting of its islands. She counted the seats and rowing boats but had to be content with an estimate of its bird population.

Miss Preece must have had a good laugh at 3B's expense. Their artistic efforts were plans rather than views. Margie's lake resembled nothing so much as a limp Rugby football flattened at one end and bulging at the other. No detail was omitted. Several islands covered with shrubbery, a number of little brown rowing boats and even microscopic swans and ducks were faithfully represented. The dirty concrete path shone pristine white and imagination had transformed the muddy grey water to Mediterranean blue.

"Stroke six gathers, then bring your work to me!"

Into the queue they crept one by one, trembling as for the guillotine.

3B were making dustcaps, articles which are not only obsolete now but were nearly so then. The cap was gathered into a broad band which was then embroidered! Every single gather had to be stroked carefully into place with the point of a needle. Margie never mastered this art and even Auntie, a dressmaker herself, thought Miss Preece unnecessarily fussy.

Each child designed her own pattern for the embroidery on the band. Margie produced a set of complicated motifs, each consisting of a circle inside a diamond inside a square; they were linked by a fussy network of intersecting lines decorated with leaves for good measure. What she hadn't taken into account was the length of time it would take to embroider this masterpiece. Long after everybody but the duds had finished, she was still struggling on. The band became so puckered that even a final pressing failed to iron out all the creases.

In contrast the pattern Clare had designed was simplicity itself, being no more than a wavy horizontal line with satin-stitch diamonds placed alternatively above and below it. Not only was her dustcap finished long before Margie's but the completed work looked neat and crisp in contrast with her rival's wrinkled muddle.

Clare met **her** Nemesis, however, when 3B started knitting on four needles. Here Margie had the advantage for both Mother and Grannie were indefatigable knitters of socks. There was seldom a moment when Grannie had no piece of knitting in her hand, and she and Mother had seen to it that Margie acquired some elementary skill in the craft. She could cast on, knit and seam, and even cast off. She also knew how to decrease, either by knitting two stitches together or by slipping a stitch and passing it over the next one: this process was indispensable in turning the heel of a sock.

Her friend Clare came from no such advantageous knitting background. She was further handicapped as the wool she had brought from home was black, so her stitches were more difficult to see than anyone else's.

Came the dreaded moment when she and Margie and two other girls were summoned to Miss Preece's desk for instruction in the tricky art of turning the heel. Clare was made doubly nervous by the conviction that the martinet had never accepted her and was eager for her downfall. So, while Margie and the others managed to follow the teacher's instructions, Clare struggled and blundered under the gimlet eye, miscounted, dropped stitches and, when the Gorgon's wrath at last descended, dissolved in floods of tears. Years later Margie could still recall the expression of gloating triumph on the teacher's face as she snatched from Clare's shaking hands the pathetic scrap of knitting. Soaked with bitter tears every needlework lesson, it was, needless to say, never finished.

Katie and Margie acted as monitors for most of the two years they spent in Miss Preece's class. They made an unlikely though complementary pair, Margie unhandy but conscientious where Katie was capable but slap-dash.

There was plenty for them to do. The class sat at benches, not desks, so every morning pens, pencils and rulers, exercise books and blotting paper had to be given out. From time to time there was the messy job of refilling inkwells and replacing them in their appointed holes in the bench tops to be negotiated.

Slate pencils with a squeak to set the nerves jangling and cracked slates with chipped wooden frames were handed out, not without a certain amount of favouritism, for Mental Arithmetic. Using slates was economical, of course, for the work could be rubbed out and the slates used over and over again. They were handy for cheating, too, as a dab from a licked finger would obliterate any mistake, but a temerity bordering on lunacy was required for trying **that** on in Miss Preece's class.

Every Friday afternoon Katie and Margie solemnly carried the half dozen large aspidistras from the classroom windowsill to the washbowls and removed a thick layer of West Riding muck from their glossy leaves.

At the end of the year Miss Preece rewarded them, to their utter amazement, with a box of chocolates apiece. The boxes were brilliant orange with a black cat on the lid and must have contained a quarter of a pound. As chocolates were a treat kept for Christmas, a present of the Crown jewels couldn't have delighted them more.

Anticipating the Christmas party was more of a thrill than the event itself. The word **party** was a misnomer to start with, as the children simply sat in their accustomed places to eat instead of work. The classroom was festooned beforehand with streamers and decorations provided by the girls and in this unusually gay atmosphere even Miss Preece mellowed. But only a little. The operation still had to be carried through with Draconian precision.

The cakes and sandwiches the children had brought from home were set out on large plates on a white-damask-covered trestle table at the front of the classroom. Paper serviettes were handed round and placed on the benches in lieu of plates. Cups weren't required as there was nothing to drink.

Miss Preece then marched round with the plates of food, one after another, beginning with sandwiches and ending with cakes. You could almost say the operation took place to numbers. There was no choice. You took what was profferred and only when a plate had gone the rounds till it was empty did another begin to circulate. The choosing and eating was all done under Miss Preece's eagle eye.

Miss Preece had a heart somewhere though, as far as 3B were concerned, it was buried deep under a layer of the millstone grit she was always talking about. Had she been more attractive in person and more good-humoured in manner, her relationship with her class might have been transformed.

Yet with her iron discipline and dogged thoroughness she was able not only to teach the three Rs and lay a magnificent groundwork of general knowledge but also to exert over her pupils an influence that would last a lifetime.

Chapter Seventeen
The Scholarship

Needlework, Poetry, Music and even Geography were, of course, mere sidelines. The subjects that really mattered were those tested for the dreaded "scholarship": Arithmetic, "Mental", Composition and Dictation, together with an intelligence test taken without even a trial run.

Every morning after the statutory Scripture lesson 4B, as they had now become, got down to the serious business of Mental. Ten questions were fired in rapid succession and each child wrote on her slate the answers only. All working had to be done in the head.

A typical question might be: "Write down the cost of a dozen yards of ribbon at three-ha'pence a yard" or "If oranges are sold at five for sixpence, how many would you get for a florin?"

Speed was all-important: time and tide and Miss Preece starting on the next question waited for no-one. Short cuts assumed great importance and the martinet drummed these incessantly into her charges. When multiplying by twelve, call the pence shillings; when multiplying by twenty, call the shillings pounds. To multiply by twenty-five, add two noughts and divide by four. It was vital to know the value of a florin and a guinea, and the number of units in a dozen, a score and a gross, for the questions were larded with these strange amounts.

Tables up to "twelve times" were learned by heart, recited day after day in a monotonous sing-song and tested often. Heaven help the wretch who couldn't remember one of the tricky bits like "Seven nines are sixty-three" or "Twelve elevens make a hundred and thirty-two"! When Miss Preece was in a vile mood, everyone with fewer than full marks for Mental or Tables (often the whole class) was lined up for a stinging blow on the palm from her stout stick.

Arithmetic proper followed: long multiplication and division, vulgar fractions, decimals, land measurement, the metric system, problems and so on. More tables had to be mastered: long and square measure, capacity and avoirdupois. It was essential to know, for example, that a hundred and twelve pounds made one hundredweight; four pecks one bushel; five and a half yards one rod, pole or perch; and four thousand eight hundred and forty square yards one acre.

The welcome but short-lived relief of playtime was followed by a session of Spelling, Grammar and Composition. At least ten new words were learned every week for the inevitable spelling test with the inevitable painful sequel for all those with less than eight right.

Miss Preece considered writing a composition was impossible without a sound basis of grammar. One must be able to distinguish between the eight different parts of speech: **nouns,** proper and common, which were simply names; **pronouns,** which stood in their stead, and **adjectives** which described both: **verbs** or "doing" words, and **adverbs** which described them: and last of all, little words with long names like **conjunctions** (joining words), **prepositions** (leaning words) and **interjections** (exclaiming words).

The rules of Composition as set forth by Miss Preece were inflexible. The subject might vary from "Too many cooks spoil the broth", through "A day in the life of a penny" to an account of a shopping expedition in town with half-a-crown (untold wealth!) to spend. But the format was always the same. A composition consisted of five paragraphs of which the first was the introduction, the second the development, the third the climax, the fourth the unravelling and the last the conclusion.

Nor did the marking scheme vary. Ten marks were awarded for handwriting, ten for spelling, ten for grammar, ten for punctuation and twenty for the subject matter, making a grand total of sixty. A mark was ruthlessly deducted for every mistake. Thus, in theory at least, it was possible for a genius with a poor grasp of spelling and syntax to plummet to a mark below zero whilst a bore possessed of a faultless technique could score at least forty for five paragraphs of tedium.

On the results of the scholarship examination hung one's chance of free secondary education up to the age of sixteen.

"Stand up, all the girls who hope to go to a secondary school!"

Miss Preece was on the warpath again.

Eight or nine sheepish victims would shuffle reluctantly to their feet, bracing themselves for the impending onslaught, while the rest (the less talented or perhaps less fortunate) relaxed in smug anticipation of getting their own back at the expense of the "clever" girls.

"**You'll** never get there!" Miss Preece would prophesy, pointing her stick at some luckless wretch and launching into a diatribe that teemed with scathing comments.

Of the four single-sex schools open to the successful applicants, Miss Preece seemed to favour the nearest, Belle Vue, which was at the time held in high esteem. But the rumour that she herself had been educated there was never confirmed.

Superior to all was the independent Bradford Grammar School for Girls which accepted fee-paying pupils only. In exceptional cases the local authority would pay the fees for a particularly talented child from one of its elementary schools. A **Grammar School scholarship** was indeed a prize!

One of Dad's customers at the shop was a bespoke tailor of Scottish origin who had fathered ten children and was consequently as poor as a church mouse. The eldest of his brood, Sandy, had been awarded such a scholarship and, as his father was never tired of telling Dad, was doing brilliantly at the Boys' Grammar School.

Although she never mentioned it and in any case doubted her ability to get there, Margie hankered for the Grammar School in secret. The attitude adopted by Miss Preece to a Grammar School scholarship was ambivalent: as a token of excellence on the one hand, it was a prize to be coveted by pupil and teacher alike; on the other, as the means of entry to a privileged establishment, it was to be spurned by folk of sturdy independence.

Nancy, a slight, dark girl with the wistful eyes of a faun, once incautiously admitted that, if she passed the exam., her parents intended to apply for a place at the Grammar School. Though she was one of the best pupils, she had never been top of the class, and Miss Preece's scorn knew no bounds. By the time she had finished, it was plain to the whole of 4B that the proverbial camel negotiating the eye of a needle stood an infinitely greater chance of success than did the presumptuous and by now tearful Nancy laying siege to so prestigious a bastion of learning.

On the fateful day in March, 1927, Margie set off for school with Dick's lordly dictum, "**She'll** never get a scholarship!" ringing in her ears.

The events of the day passed in a confused blur. The dose of Mental was administered by no less a person than the fearsome head teacher herself. Arithmetic followed. Margie hadn't time to finish the paper.

In the afternoon they were faced with the dreaded Intelligence Test. Afterwards Margie could recall only one question: "Place the following words in strict alphabetical order: spectacles, splendid, spiteful, sparkle, spreading."

They all began with 's'. They all began with 'sp'! What to do? In despair Margie did the only thing she could think of and arranged the words according to their third letter: sparkle, spectacles, spiteful, splendid, spreading.

She returned home convinced of failure.

Aeons crawled by without any news. Glad tidings came at long last to Millicent and Mabel in 4A, Katie and Winnie, Nancy, Clare and Margie: they had all been awarded scholarships.

Dad had to fill in a form, stating his choice of schools in order of preference. When Margie brought her secret into the open and announced that she wanted the Grammar School to be her first choice, there was general consternation. Dad, always so ready to extol Sandy's merits, didn't seem to have a like confidence in his own daughter's talents while Dick hastened to brand the Grammar School as the seat of snobbery.

The only one to sympathise with Margie was Mother, anxious as always to do her best for her children. She knew from experience how it felt to hanker after things you could never possess. But even **she** had to point out the brutal facts of the case.

Girls who went to the Grammar School came from the **upper ten,** that is, from well-to-do families living in their own houses in a better neighbourhood. They would have more pocket money than Margie; she would feel inferior; she might not be able to make friends. The school uniform would be more expensive than that for Belle Vue and there would be all sorts of extras Mother and Dad simply couldn't afford.

Margie knew in her heart that Mother was right and that it was best for all the members of a family to go to the same school and have similar opportunities. But it was a bitter pill to swallow. She vented her disappointment in a fit of the sulks and said that, if they wouldn't apply to the Grammar School, then they could just put down "Belle Vue" and leave the rest of the form blank.

Which is what they did.

When the Drummond Road girls were summoned to Belle Vue for interview, they wasted the whole morning waiting in the crowded main hall. From the numbers present it seemed that winning a scholarship wasn't such an exceptional feat after all. It was nearly twelve before each in turn was called to the head mistress's sanctum. A bored woman with cropped silver-grey hair and a chilling manner handed Margie a sheet of paper and requested her to read aloud. A couple of minutes and it was all over. It was very disappointing. But, sitting amid the hubbub and chatter in the hallowed precincts of the Belle Vue Secondary School for Girls, she and Clare had absorbed eagerly the contents of the impressive green Honours Board above the dais. Inscribed in letters of gold for all the world to see were the names and achievements of the distinguished women who had been educated there during the fifty years since its foundation.

In awe and reverence Margie made a resolve: if she were accepted as a pupil at Belle Vue, then one day **her** name and achievements would be emblazoned in one of the waiting spaces.

Long before the summer term drew to its close everything was settled. Millicent, Mabel, Katie, Winnie, Clare and Margie were to go to Belle Vue. Margie tried hard to suppress a pang of resentment when the news broke that Nancy had been accepted for the Grammar School. Miss Preece made her stand in front of the class like a delinquent and informed her that she had only got in because others whose names were higher up the list hadn't applied.

So at the end of four years the cream was skimmed off into the secondary schools. The less fortunate pupils were to remain at Drummond Road for a further three years, passing through Standards Five, Six and Seven before leaving for the world of work the day they became fourteen.

Was it Miss Preece or Miss Parkin who told Mother and Clare's mother in confidence on the last day of term that heading the scholarship list for the whole city were the names of Clare and Margie? Miss Preece's pupils hadn't let her down after all. Drummond Road had done it again!

Chapter Eighteen

Swings and Roundabouts

"Collop Monday, Pancake Tuesday, Ash Wednesday, Fritter Thursday, Fish Friday." So said Grannie who was knowledgeable and superstitious about festivals.

Collops were overlapping slices of potato roasted in the oven in a tin of fat so that the edges became crisp by the centres stayed soft. This delicious alternative to plain boiled or mashed always appeared on Collop Monday but otherwise all too rarely.

The ash of Ash Wednesday might be a sprinkling of ashes on the forehead as far as the church was concerned. To Grannie it was "hash", a meat and potato stew served on the first day of Lent. **Hash** Wednesday, in fact!

Shrove Tuesday had become a regular holiday by the time Margie started school. The fortunate secondary schools even took Monday as well and called it half-term.

Shrovetide brought the first stirrings of Spring in the corporate child consciousness. On Shrove Tuesday, as if by magic, out into the back street came all the whips and tops.

The top was made of solid wood; it can best be described as a thick cylinder mounted on a short, inverted, metal-tipped cone. Dick's favourite was a squat, lumbering, dark grey monster christened Jumbo. On its flat round top he chalked concentric rings ranging through the spectrum from vermilion to violet. A leather whip was coiled round the continuous groove in Jumbo's side, then pulled away at lightning speed to set him in motion.

As Jumbo swayed and hummed, vibrated and leapt to the lash of the whip, his coloured top showed white, thus proving, to Dick's satisfaction at any rate, that light could be split into the seven colours of the rainbow and vice versa. To Margie Jumbo's spinning top looked a dirty grey, but who was she to challenge the Physics master at Belle Vue?

Good Friday wasn't a general holiday although by then the schools had broken up for Easter. The woollen mills worked a five-and-a-half-day week and didn't close down for the weekend till Saturday noon. Many millhands were on short time, though, and Uncle Walter would usually call round because he was 'lakin''.

"By! There's a good smell!" he'd exclaim as he walked into the kitchen. For besides the usual Friday bread, Mother and Grannie would be baking hot cross buns, as well he knew, and wouldn't let him return home empty-handed. They weren't the paltry little buns on sale today, but great "long buns" bursting with currants and spice and peel. Before they were put in the oven, a cross, with the upright twice as long as the crossbar, was cut into them with a sharp knife.

To make up for the loss of Good Friday, both Monday and Tuesday were public holidays. Hundreds would flock to the moors on Easter Monday, not by car but on foot. The ten-mile route through Shipley Glen to Dick Hudson's well-known inn and thence over the springy peat into Ilkley was so jammed with humanity that it resembled Manningham Lane when a crowd of football supporters were just "loosing" from a Cup-tie at Valley Parade.

The family never went beyond Shipley Glen. As all the trams were packed, they had to walk, the children somewhat unwillingly, taking the short cut through the park and under the Norman archway into the Keighley Road. Some distance further on, the crowd turned right at Victoria Road as if by common consent. A short walk brought them into Saltaire.

It was much cleaner than Bradford. The mill was surrounded by superior dwelling houses and other attractive buildings of honey-coloured stone which clustered on the banks of the River Aire. But Margie had eyes only for the stone lions which crouched, two on either side of the parapet where the road bridged the river.

Dad had said that when the lions heard the church clock strike the hour, they would get up and roar. The prospect terrified Margie. She gripped her parents' hands tight, for the time wanted only a few minutes to three.

"Hurry! hurry!" she begged, aghast at the bland unconcern on their faces. Dad was even laughing. She quickened her pace, trying without success to pull them along with her. The danger area safely passed, she looked back, breathless and fearful, still clinging to their hands for safety. But by the time the clock struck the hour, they were too far off either to see the lions rise and yawn and stretch, or to hear them roar.

It was a tiring climb up the rough path to the glen but there was always a long queue for the Glen Tramway. Occasionally they would join it but more often they had to walk.

111

A ride on the Glen Tramway was the height of bliss. Each tram consisted of several linked open cars with rows of slatted seats. It sped up the gentle wooded incline as if by magic, along wires which hummed and sang down below. Half-way up you could count on the excitement of meeting the "down" tram (almost empty in mid-afternoon) for the two cars were counterpoised in some way.

Everything happened at Peel Park on Whit Monday. Peel Park **Gay-la** (as every Bradfordian called it) was an annual event and attending it was Dick and Margie's ultimate ambition. There was a "tide" with stalls and roundabouts, a brass band, teas and pop and ice cream, races for the children and dancing in the evening for the adults.

But the paramount attraction was the balloon. So far the children had had to content themselves with watching it go up from a distance. Long before six o'clock, the time scheduled for the ascent, they would toil up the hill to join the knot of observers already gathered at the vantage point on Heaton Road.

The green patch just below the horizon to the right of centre was Peel Park and one could pick out, without too much difficulty, the white blob of the by now fully inflated balloon.

Somehow it always went up when you weren't looking. You stared and stared with fierce concentration at the white blur, immobile against its green background. The sun got in your eyes; you put up a hand to shield them from the glare, shifted your weight from one leaden foot to the other, glanced away for a split second and ... the crowd yelled, the balloon was airborne and you'd missed the magic moment.

All was not lost for there was more excitement to come. Look! a tiny white speck has dropped from the balloon. Down, down it plummets, then suddenly steadies and blossoms into a white flower which drifts gently to earth. A few seconds later it is followed by another and sometimes even by a third.

Each time the suspense is agonising. You hold your breath in case the parachute should fail to open and the gallant passenger hurtle to his death.

Gradually the white blob which is the balloon becomes smaller and smaller until it can no longer be distinguished. It is time to go home. Tomorrow an account in the **Telegraph and Argus** will tell you where the parachutists and balloon eventually landed, the latter often sixty or seventy miles off.

112

One never-to-be-forgotten year Dick and Margie actually went to the Gay-la. There was no convenient tram but with fares so expensive (tuppence for adults and a penny for children) the family always walked, anyhow. It was a long way down into the valley, across the canal and railway line and up the hill on the other side. An ever-growing crowd of weary, jostling figures struggled along in the dust and heat towards the park gates.

Dad paid their entrance money and obtained programmes. Straight ahead, like an enormous mushroom growing in the grass, rose a smooth greyish-white hemisphere. Closer inspection showed the balloon to be distinctly grubby and even patched in places. The monster billowed and swayed as it sucked in the gas which was gradually plumping out its creases. Piles of sandbags lay on the ground. Some were already attached to the giant but many more would be needed to hold it down later.

At one of the stalls they were selling gas-filled balloons, small coloured replicas of the monster which was still absorbing gas on the green. Each was covered with mesh to which a little wicker basket was attached. They were very dear at eightpence each but Mother bought two with the money Auntie had given her to spend on the children.

"Keep tight hold of the string," shouted the vendor, "or the gas will carry them away!"

Just before six they took up a position on the edge of the crowd round the balloon. Dad lifted Margie up so that she could see. The huge silver-grey sphere, now twice its former size, was bucking and swaying like a live creature. Several men, muffled in caps and greatcoats in spite of the heat, were climbing into its big wicker basket. One by one the restraining sandbags were unhooked and in their stead, groups of sweating volunteers strained at the ropes. Backwards and forwards they surged, shuffling and slithering on the greasy turf in their struggle to hold down the captive giant.

Suddenly she was away. As the breeze caught her, she pitched and tossed, climbing ever higher with the basket swaying below. Two white parachutes drooped from hooks on either side of the silken globe and dangling from the trailing threads of each was a large metal ring. On one of these sat the graceful figure of the balloonist's daughter wearing a dark costume. From the ring of the other parachute her seventeen-year-old brother, in a navy suit with white sailor collar, hung by his hands, twisting and twirling like the passengers on the flying chairs, as the balloon floated away into the sky.

There was an audible gasp from the crowd as, with a dextrous flexing of his arms, he pulled himself up to a sitting position on the ring and gave them a triumphant wave of the hand. Margie's heart thudded fit to burst, then almost stopped as the girl's parachute dropped from the balloon like a stone.

Down, down it fell, the crowd holding their breath until, sighing with relief, they saw the white parasol puff out and, swaying gracefully from side to side, continue a more leisurely descent somewhere beyond the belt of trees.

In a few seconds the boy dropped from a now greater height and once again hearts stopped till the plummeting figure was checked by the opening of the second white umbrella.

The two parachutes coming slowly down looked so close that the crowd began to stampede across the grass, thinking they might land on the edge of the park.

"They'll be miles off!" was Dad's judgment as he set Margie down. She relaxed her grip and the scarlet balloon, covered with golden mesh, floated away over the heads of the crowd.

Dick was more fortunate or more tenacious and managed to get **his** safely home. When at last he let go of the string, it floated along the passage, up three flights of stairs, and came to rest touching the attic ceiling.

Two of the traditional festivals still observed in the nineteen-twenties were Manningham Tide, held in late spring, and Bowling Tide in mid-August. To the children the word "tide" was synonymous with "fair".

Manningham Tide struggled on in the twenties as an emaciated relic of its pre-war self. It was held on a cinder-patch of waste ground along Drummond Road, not far from school. Margie scarcely noticed the mud and litter underfoot, the shifty-eyed tinkers and their grubby, tousled children. To her all was glamour and excitement, from the garish painting on the horse-drawn caravans to the deafening blare of the music and raucous shouts of the pedlars.

There were stalls where you could buy brandy snaps, hot peas and pies, or tripe and cowheel; tents where the future would be revealed; rifle ranges, coconut shies, boxing booths and, of course, roundabouts. Dick wore out his pants whizzing round the helter-skelter while Margie jogged sedately up and down on the staid horses of the merry-go-round.

114

The children had never been to the bigger and better fair at Bowling on the other side of town. To them "Bowling Tide" meant the culmination of the summer holidays for it was the week when Dad was off work. A week off was a mixed blessing for there were no holidays with pay. Somehow the money for the week's food and rent had to be found so there was little to spare for treats and outings.

Bowling Tide week was a byword for bad weather. But one year every day of the holiday week dawned fine and warm.

The family ... Dad, Mother, Dick, Margie, Baby (who was now four) and Auntie Annie ... went by train to spend a whole week in Bridlington or Brid, as Dad always called it. You could tell from the way Dad spoke that Brid was very special.

The first special thing happened before they had even quitted the railway station. A boy came up and said to Dad, "Carry your bags, sir?" He knew where to go the minute Dad told him the address and carried two of the cases all the way to the boarding house. Apart from being made of brick instead of stone, it was quite like the house in Leamington Street, even to the outside double-you.

Each day Mother bought their food and the landlady cooked it. They sat together at a big table in the middle of the front room. A jolly, middle-aged couple from Armley in Leeds had the small table in the bay window. Each table was permanently covered with a white cloth and had a cruet in the middle.

Another special thing about Brid was the range of exciting things in the shops. Even the bread was different. It came in long cylindrical rolls with grooved sides and tasted quite different from the loaves at home. You could also buy buckets and spades; postcards with pictures of fat, red-cheeked women sitting on donkeys; and brightly coloured celluloid windmills to stick on top of your sand castle. There was nothing like that in the Bradford shops.

Dad played cricket on the sands with Dick and took Margie paddling with his trousers rolled up to the knee. Margie wore a pair of crackly, checked waterproof waders with a bib top and voluminous, uncomfortable elasticated bloomers. Though very special, the sea was also cold and frightening and the gritty feel of damp sand between the toes most unpleasant. She clung tight to Dad's hand as the creeping tongues of foam licked round her feet.

The most special thing of all was building sand castles. Dad and Dick made a beauty with tunnels and turrets and ramparts and a moat.

It was thrilling to watch the incoming tide surge into the moat and through the tunnels, gradually but inexorably encroaching till the proud bastion was reduced to a soggy mound, crumbling forlorn amid the victorious waves.

Making a castle was difficult. For her part Margie could imagine no occupation more satisfying than filling a bucket with damp sand, banging the top hard and flat with the back of a spade and up-ending it to form a perfect sand pie.

They went away next summer as well but the holiday was an anti-climax compared with the one in Brid. This time the family split up. Margie and Baby went with Mother and Auntie in a taxi to a place called Tong to stay with Cousin Annie, an elderly relative the children had never met before. Wherever Tong was, it certainly wasn't the seaside. This rankled in Margie's mind for Dad had taken Dick to Morecambe, which certainly was.

Cousin Annie lived in a poky cottage covered with roses and Virginia creeper. Tong was depressingly quiet and there was nothing to do. Every morning they walked to the village where the old stocks and mounting block were of little interest to the two children. They would stop outside the large, wrought-iron gates of Tong Hall and peer through the railings at the peacocks strutting in the grounds. Auntie said they would spread their tails into a beautiful fan of blue and turquoise feathers but though they watched every day, it didn't happen once.

Margie considered the journey home the best part of the holiday. Cousin Annie had given them a bunch of sweet peas, stocks and gypsophila from her tiny garden and their intoxicating fragrance filled the taxi.

Dick had come back from Morecambe with a sprained ankle, a by-product of cricket on the sands. With his leg swathed in interesting layers of white bandage and propped up on a cushion, he sat issuing orders and expecting (and getting) everybody's solicitous attention. He was obviously enjoying himself.

There was no justice, thought Margie. She put the flowers in a big kitchen jug but by the next morning they were dead.

Chapter Nineteen

Winter Festivals

"Remember, remember the fifth of November,
Gunpowder treason and plot,
When Guido, poor feller,
Was nabbed in the cellar,
And afterwards caught it red-hot!"

(Traditional, altered)

Dick and Margie were delighted to find in **The Magnet** this new and ribald version of the familiar rhyme. For there was no such thing in the West Riding as Bonfire Night or Guy Fawkes Night. The great event of the autumn was known then, and is to this day, by its correct title, Plot.

For weeks beforehand a gang of boys from the back street had spent its Saturday afternoons chumping in Heaton Woods, returning laden with branches of trees and chunks of wood to be stored in somebody's back yard against the festival. As Dad was working on Saturdays, he heard little about the chumping expeditions but he would certainly not have approved of them. Mother was uneasy about the gang being led by an older boy whose reckless behaviour was admired and copied by the rest. Dick would come home with thrilling accounts of trespassing on private land and hair's-breadth escapes from angry farmers, but he was careful to keep his mouth shut when Dad was about.

The night before Plot was known as Mischief Night. Groups of excited children, keyed up for the events of the morrow, would chase round the neighbourhood, knocking on doors and running away, sometimes even daring to throw a lighted rip-rap through a letter-box. The Harrop family were good at boasting of their adventures on Mischief Night. Mother wouldn't allow her children out to take part in such goings-on although, when Dick was older, he usually managed to sneak off on some pretext to join the gang and share in its dare-devil exploits.

The bonfire was built the day before in the middle of the back street. It was so big that even pedestrians could hardly get by, so for once people had to use their front doors. No vehicle could pass, be it coal-cart, milk-float or greengrocer's van. Even Salt Jim and the yest man with their little handcarts had to make a detour.

Plot was a community event and most parents took part. Mothers made parkin and treacle toffee and provided potatoes for baking in the embers. Fathers superintended the tricky business of getting the fire going and trying to prevent accidents. Dick and the other boys rushed about, putting rockets in bottles and setting off rip-raps and ha'penny thunderflashes.

Girls and younger children, hands and feet frozen though their faces were scorched by the heat of the fire, twirled sparklers and red and green Bengal lights, sucked Plot toffee, gazed open-mouthed at a whizzing Catherine wheel pinned to someone's clothes stoop, gaped at the gold and silver rain and popping coloured stars of a Roman candle, and craned their necks to follow the blazing trail slashed across the velvet sky by a rocket.

When the fire was old, potatoes were placed among the embers. There is nothing quite like the taste and texture of a potato baked in a Plot bonfire, as Margie soon discovered, gingerly removing the hot, bitter black skin from the outside and nibbling cautiously at the hard, raw interior.

Finally the guy, a grotesque straw figure in somebody's old suit and battered hat, was hoisted to the summit of the fire and consumed in a hideous public spectacle.

A series of large black rings on the cobbles of the street marked the sites of successive annual commemorations of "gunpowder treason and plot". There was trouble one year when the heat from the fire blistered the paint on the wooden doors of two of the nearest middens and all but set them alight.

By the time she was seven Margie had started her piano lessons. Miss Hodgson came every Wednesday evening for what became the most miserable half-hour of Margie's week.

She was looking forward with glee to missing her next lesson and simply couldn't believe it when Miss Hodgson told Auntie that she would come round as usual.

"But she can't!" Margie cried, aghast. "It's Plot!" It was like being expected to go to school on Christmas Day.

All through the week she hoped against hope that authority would relent. She pleaded with Mother, Auntie, Georgie (who was sympathetic but powerless to intervene) and even Dad, but all in vain.

When Dick got ready to go out with his fireworks, Margie started putting on her coat but was told she would only get dirty and must stay in and wait for Miss Hodgson.

It was a sullen, resentful child who scowled and thumped her way through her pieces, listening, not to the wrong notes she was playing, but to the distant shouts of laughter, the sudden hiss and crackle of a rocket, the sputter of a Roman candle or the rat-a-tat of a rip-rap. The familiar acrid smell of Plot seeped into the front room, making her eyes sting and water and bringing a choking sensation to her throat.

By the time the lesson was over it was nearly her bedtime. With nose pressed to the steamy window of the back room, where the glow from the fire was still visible and the shouts of Dick and the other revellers could clearly be heard, she experienced the first real tragedy of her life.

The weekly baking had gone on for much longer than usual and dusk was falling. Mother was covering buns with icing, then dipping them in coconut, an unusual occupation which was a source of wonder and delight to four-year-old Margie. As she trimmed the pastry round the individual mince pie tins, Grannie was humming a strange and beautiful song about jelly, Margie's favourite food. There was an indefinable air of excitement and anticipation abroad.

Georgie came stamping into the kitchen, letting in an icy blast.

"It's snowing!" he announced, picking Margie up and lifting a corner of the lace curtain to reveal the soft flakes drifting gently down. "Perhaps we shall have a white Christmas after all."

It was the first time Margie had seen snow. It was also her first conscious realisation of Christmas. From then on, that season of the year was magic.

To begin with, there were special songs you were only allowed to sing around Christmas time. She soon learned that the one about jelly started off,

"Hark! the herald angels sing",
and continued,

"With th' angelic host proclaim
Christ is born in Bethlehem".

Another favourite was "While shepherds watched their flocks by night". Dick had his own irreverent version when Grannie wasn't about.

119

"While shepherds washed their socks by night,
All seated round the tub,
A bar of Hudson's soap came down
And with it they did scrub."

He had his own parody of **The Mistletoe Bough,** an affecting song
of Grannie's about the mysterious disappearance of a Christmas bride
during a game of **Hide and Seek** on her wedding night. The mystery
wasn't solved till an old oak chest came to light years later, when
the bridegroom was an old man, and its gruesome content, a
mouldering skeleton in a bridal wreath, was revealed. Quite unmoved
by the macabre nature of the tale, Dick would warble in a mock
falsetto,

"O the mistletoe bough!
Where has she mizzled to now?"

As a Christmas decoration a mistletoe bough had its limitations. Two
wooden hoops, swathed with twisted lengths of crepe paper and
interlocked at right angles, were decked with baubles and streamers,
not forgetting the bunch of mistletoe hanging from the lowest point.

Everything changed the year a long, flimsy cardboard box arrived.
It had been sent by Miss Hodgson, Margie's hated music teacher,
who now considered herself too sophisticated for a Christmas tree
and had decided to give away her decorations.

Miss Hodgson was a spoilt only daughter whose slightest wish had
always been granted. The children goggled at the contents of the box.
There were two angels, one large and one small, with flaxen curls,
blue robes and feathery white wings covered with glitter. Margie,
of course, insisted they were fairies.

A noisy red, white and blue striped trumpet engaged Dick's attention.
There was also a white celluloid horn on which perched a charming
figure of Little Boy Blue amid a pile of Christmas gifts, but Dick
dismissed it and its muted note as sissy.

A white duck with a yellow beak and a grey turkey with a red one
dangled from strings, long legs hanging limp, thin necks moving from
side to side as if they really were quacking and gobbling. Besides such
curiosities the box was heaped with shiny coloured balls and link upon
link of exotic beads, pearl and rose and silver.

It was impossible to display such a wealth of treasure on a meagre
mistletoe bough. In spite of Grannie's traditionalist grumbles, Mother
and Auntie organised a shopping expedition and came home with

120

a starkly nude artificial tree stuck in an inadequate little pot. A protesting Margie was bundled off to bed and promised a transformation in the morning.

Mother and Auntie were as good as their word. The tree now stood in a nest of crinkly red paper inside the imposing dark green pot, ornamented with large white-fronted pelicans, which usually housed an enormous aspidistra. Fairies and coloured balls, horn and trumpet and nodding birds swung from the branches which were festooned with links of glittering beads. It was like fairyland.

Father Christmas had always dealt generously with the Lumley grandchildren. In the back room stood the grey and white rocking horse with scarlet harness which he had given Dick several years ago. But Dick's taste now ran to Meccano and a fort full of tin soldiers.

When Margie was six, she was delighted with a small white piano which had a range of an octave and a half. Its obvious limitations as a serious instrument had led the following year to the start of her disastrous brief course of lessons with Miss Hodgson.

Her favourite book, the **Rainbow Annual,** featured Tiger Tim and Sunshine Susie and the other characters from her beloved Monday night comic. A series of **Wonder Books** proved popular. One year Margie was given the **Wonder Book of Children,** an illustrated manual of Social Geography, and Dick the **Wonder Book of Aircraft** which traced the brief history of flying and had pictures of biplanes, flying boats and airships, the marvels of the twenties.

Not all books were well received. Dick couldn't care less about **Young England** though it had a cover illustration of the popular Prince of Wales wearing the full feathered headdress of an Indian chief. **Tales of King Arthur,** an expensive but unsuitable choice which he ridiculed, became a favourite with Margie. She revelled in the romantic legends and beautiful coloured plates showing armoured knights on horseback and golden-haired, bejewelled damsels in flowing robes.

Later she was given its companion volume, an abridged version of Lamb's **Tales from Shakespeare.** She had been told some of the stories already by Mother, who had seen Henry Irving and Ellen Terry in many Shakespearian productions at the Theatre Royal in Bradford before her marriage. At the time Miss Preece was using proverbs as Composition subjects. She must have been surprised to find that Margie's essay based on the proverb, ''All that glitters is not gold'', was an account of the casket scene from **The Merchant of Venice.**

There was always pork for dinner on Christmas Day, preceded by Grannie's savoury pudding served with gravy. Outside a brass band played **Hail! smiling morn!** In the afternoon Uncle Arthur and Aunt Alice would arrive, and perhaps the cousins from Buttershaw on the other side of town.

Tea would be served at the table in the back room instead of in the kitchen. Boiled ham and tongue and celery and tomatoes and a stand pie were followed by tinned fruit and jelly and custard, Margie's favourite fare; mince pies, jam tarts, lemon cheese tarts, maids of honour, and spice cake with Stilton cheese.

Afterwards they would all adjourn to the front room, Grannie's seldom-used sitting room, for party games like **Stations; Nut, nut, nut;** and **Hunt the Slipper.** The last game both terrified and fascinated Margie. Though she scarcely got a touch of the slipper as the players passed it along secretly behind their backs, she lived in dread of being caught in possession and finding herself out in front, exposed to the rough and tumble and frequent whacks on the behind with it, which seemed to be the lot of the unhappy hunter.

During a lull in the excitement, boxes of dates and bowls of apples, oranges, bananas and tangerines, luxuries seldom seen in the Lumley household, would be handed round to refresh the company.

Even Grannie laughed and forgot to grumble. Perhaps she was reminded of the old days when her family were all at home, before their youthful hopes had been blighted by war and accident, mass production and unemployment.

But sooner or later someone would remember that it was long past Margie's bedtime and she would be bundled off, leaving Dick still enjoying himself downstairs.

Chapter Twenty

Farewell

1926 was the year the spring cleaning took so long. It was odd that, as late as September, drawers were still being cleared out and rooms turned upside down. Margie couldn't remember anything like it in previous years. Yet every time she complained about the confusion and muddle that seemed to have gripped the entire household, Mother put it down to the spring cleaning.

It was also odd that Dad and Mother were paying so many visits to Uncle Bill and Aunt Ada's. At least, that was where they **said** they were going whenever Margie asked. Dick was usually allowed to go with them but Margie always had to stay at home with Grannie and Auntie and Baby, even though she kept telling them how much she liked going to see Cousin Willie. Life was very unfair.

The strangest thing of all was that once she caught sight of a bucket and floorcloth and bar of soap they were taking with them. And Mother was very cross the time Margie asked her why she'd got her pinny on under her coat.

On Sunday evening, October 10th, the bombshell burst. Next Wednesday, Baby's sixth birthday, they would be leaving the familiar world of Leamington Street and never coming back. Grannie, Auntie Annie and Georgie were going to live with Uncle Bill and Aunt Ada: Mother and Dad, Dick, Margie and Baby were to move to a brand-new "Corporation house" much further away.

To say that Margie was staggered at the turning upside down of her secure little world would be an understatement. She was devastated. There were only two days left: **two days** in which to say goodbye to Grannie and Auntie and her beloved Georgie, Jack Ambler and the back street grang, the park where she spent so many happy hours, and the house itself, the only home she had ever known.

Dick took the move in his stride: after all, **he'd** been in the secret for some time and he would still be going to Belle Vue. But what of Baby, who had just completed twelve months in the infants' school, and Margie at the start of the vital scholarship year?

Mother went to see Miss Parkin. It was decided that Baby should be transferred to a school near the new house but that Margie had better continue in Miss Preece's class at Drummond Road till the end of the school year. That was how she became the lone dinner girl, eating a solitary lunch every day in the deserted classroom.

At dinnertime on Wednesday, the unlucky thirteenth, the children went home to Leamington Street for the last time. When they tumbled into the familiar kitchen it was unrecognisable. There had always been a fire, summer and winter alike, but now for the first time the grate was cold and empty.

There was no dinner, either, only pork pies which they had to eat standing as there were no chairs. They had disappeared together with the deal table, the iron mangle, the big fireguard, the two rocking chairs, even the tab rug from before the hearth.

Dick suggested a farewell tour of the house. It was the sort of romantic gesture people made in books. Margie swallowed the rest of her pie and trailed up the stairs after him.

The house looked utterly strange. It was as though they had never lived there. They went from one deserted room to another, their footsteps echoing on the bare boards.

Grannie's sitting room was an empty shell. The great carved overmantel was still there, of course, but her rosewood piano with the brass candlesticks; the red plush furniture covered with yellow crocheted antimacassars; the knick-knacks and ornaments and petit point pictures of Biblical scenes ... all had vanished. Through the curtainless windows they gazed in astonishment at the two enormous removal vans drawn up in the street outside, with Grannie's furniture and belongings in one and theirs in the other.

It was worse in the much-loved back room where they had played with their toys and listened to the gramophone with Mother and Dad on Sunday evenings. The peacock still strutted on the shabby walls but the room was bare save for an alien bicycle propped against the windowsill.

Margie looked down into the back street, still scarred with the tarry imprints of last year's, and the year before's, communal bonfires. When Plot came round in only three weeks' time, they would be far away. Never again would they play **Relievo!** or **Tin Can Squat** with the rest of the gang. When they went back to school that afternoon, they would be treading the familiar, uneven cobbles for the last time.

How could she bear it? There was an emptiness in the pit of the stomach, a sensation of hanging suspended in a limbo between two worlds. The old life had gone already, even though school would be the same for the next year. The new life had not yet started. It stretched ahead, unknown and terrifying.

Then, looking across the street at the familiar outline of Jack Ambler's house, she was suddenly gripped by a sense of purpose. After all, she told herself firmly, she was ten now: she had reached double figures. Never again would she consider anything she thought or did stupid or childish, as she had done in the past. Those days were over. She was an adult now with a rational and sensible mind. She had reached years of discretion.

Squaring her shoulders, she turned from the back street, and together she and Dick went out of the room.